Buy Smart

What you need to know when investing in UK properties

Sally Wang

Clink Street

London | New York

Published by Clink Street Publishing 2015

Copyright © 2015

First edition.

ISBN: 978-1-910782-47-7
E-Book: 978-1-910782-48-4

Printed in Great Britain by Clays Ltd, St Ives plc

Mike,

Hope you'll like this book

Sally

This book is dedicated to Tony Biesack, Ye Wang and YanRu Wei with thanks for your unconditional love, belief and support.

"When a man is tired of London, he is tired of life."

Samuel Johnson

Table of Contents

Foreword

The United Kingdom, and London specifically, has long been a favoured investment location for Chinese and overseas individuals. Since the UK's General Election in May 2015, the political and economic environment continues to be very stable and the economic growth forecasts for the next five years look most positive and remain amongst the best in Europe.

London is booming and is considered to be a safe place to do business in, with a myriad of property professionals available to support you and your investments.

The UK is very much open to international business and welcomes foreign direct investment, as clearly demonstrated by the huge number of overseas funded construction projects completed during the past 20 years. The UK also has a solid reputation as a safe and secure base for international investment.

Divided into three sections, this book is designed to help overseas buyers to have a more enjoyable and productive buying experience. This can be done by teaching you clearly how to do research and how to understand the buying procedure; the types of properties, what to expect before entering the legal process. Including such things as 'what will happen once you decide to buy' and it will also help you after the completion process, with vitally important points such as renting out the property, or selling on to make a profit — in fact this book covers the complete cycle.

We all need to know that property investments can be risky and that is why it is essential to work with reputable professionals. The rewards can of course be outstanding, but like any investment, things can go very wrong — so you have to be covered from day one. I believe that this book is a fantastic tool to help and support you. Therefore, I am delighted to support this fantastic production.

My own enthusiastic interest in China began many years ago, which resulted in my first visit to the Chinese mainland and Hong Kong back in 1995 with my son The Hon Richard Evans. We often talk about our amazing and unique experiences, travelling through China at that time and the absolutely tremendous progress that the PRC has made since. I am very much involved in Foreign Direct Investment (FDI) and regularly visit countries to advise governments and companies on this vitally important area.

I hope that you enjoy this wonderful insight and congratulate Sally for her hard work and initiative — which I am sure will enhance commercial relations between our two great countries.

Warmest regards

David - Lord Evans of Watford
Non-Executive Director - ACE Funding Ltd - London.

Preface

Oct 2001: I was on the plane to London for the next chapter of my life. Like many other Chinese undergraduates at the time, I was here to pursue a further education in order to better myself. A few years later, after completion of my degree and a job that offered me a work permit, I was lucky enough to stay and go a little bit further.

In China, we have a saying: "settle down and work happily". Settling down mainly refers to having a place of your own, which was extremely challenging for me at the time. As a young graduate without much money and a most basic salary, there was no way for me to afford a place in London. My only option was to buy a small property somewhere else in the UK, rent it out, use the rental income to cover part of my rental expenses in London; save up a big chunk of my salary, (hoping the price of my property would go up at some point), sell it, make some profit; and then I might have a chance to climb up the property ladder here in the UK.

Well, that was the bold master plan which I could come up at the time and I was lucky enough to actually pull it off!

But the stress that I went through, along with the fear and worry I brought to my parents at that time, left such an emotional mark on me that a seed of writing a book to help people like me was embedded in my mind.

I can't tell you how much I wished there were someone or some book out there at the time, which could have helped me with my buying process or answer at least one of my questions. I can't tell you how surprised I was purely at the fact that I was still sane after the completion of the deal. At one point, I thought I had developed split personality condition. I was young and foreign, my English was OK but not fantastic, my knowledge of buying property was next to zero, I had no friends around me who had property buying experience and I had no one to go to for any advice, let alone professional help. But the only thing I kept telling myself was that I could not show my lack of knowledge in front of the agents, because my biggest fear was that if they saw through me and realised that I was just a silly young foreign woman who knew nothing about buying a property, they could just show me any rubbish stock and sell me the worst property.

I knew that was my biggest fear and it was that major concern that kept me awake at night. I was so busy worrying about my own concerns that I did not even have the time or energy to ask what was keeping my mum awake at night during those few months; until recently that is, when I started to write this book.

"Where there is a will, there is a way". My way to conquer my fear was to hide it. I chose to hide my fear, my inexperience and my zero knowledge on buying a property. I also created two rules for myself to follow.

Rule number one: I must appear calm and look thoughtful.

Rule number two: never give them a straight answer, buy some time for myself, and go home to do some research on the internet.

I wanted to appear SMART, although I knew in reality I was everything but SMART.

If that sale hadn't completed as fast as it did back then (thankfully, I was lucky enough to find a good solicitor who did a great job in completing the deal) even I could not have predicted what would happen to me. To live in constant stress and in a dark situation was no fun. I remember that every time I needed to make a decision, I was screaming inside for help. Which solicitor to use, whether to do the survey or not, where do I find proof of income; it went on and on and on; everything seemed so daunting and exhausting. I felt as if I was going through a pitch-dark tunnel on my own without knowing when I would reach the end of it and see the light.

The Internet did not help that much either. First of all, I could not find a single complete resource in my own language to direct me and give me everything (or close to it) that I needed to know about buying a property in the UK; secondly, there was so much noise and information on the websites just around one topic, I did not know who to trust or even what the references would be for me to use in order to decide whether to trust a piece of information or not; thirdly, there were no real time case studies, real stories that I could relate to; and last but not least, there were not many Chinese people at that time who were buying properties in the UK and there were not many real estate professionals around who could speak Chinese.

I suppose that experience made me want to do something to change this, to improve the situation, to help people like me, to make the lives of people like my parents easier.

Shortly afterwards, I followed my passion and started working in the property industry. That opened the door to an increasing number of international buyers, especially the Chinese.

If I have to use three words to describe the Chinese buyers, they would be "different, indecisive and demanding".

As a person who was born and brought up in China and then spent 14 years here in the UK, I can see, feel and understand the difference easily. The difference starts from the initial thinking process and buying behaviour to the way they communicate. The difference is profound and has deep roots in their long established cultures.

When I was giving a speech to over 100 Chinese investors in the Four Seasons Hotel, Canary Wharf on "Why Invest in East London" in winter 2014, I chose to focus my topic on one key element: the change. The changes that I had witnessed with my own eyes in the past decade were enormous, and I knew that was just a tiny part of a big picture.

On one of my business trips to Shanghai in 2014, a TV programme that I happened to watch stunned me with its facts and figures. The latest Fortune 500 report shows that in 2014, 100 of the top 500 companies in the world were from China, ranking number two globally. This is in stark contrast to the early 1950s, when the total income of the biggest 500 Chinese companies could not even match the turnover of General Motors at the time. China's GDP has increased by 122 times from 1953 to 2013. Now we cannot use years, months or even days to describe the speed and scale of China's growth; we need to use seconds. Every single second, the Chinese spend 570,000RMB and three Chinese people travel abroad. 2013 and 2014 have also seen a number of big Chinese companies' activities in London's property market, such as ABP's £1 billion deal on Royal Albert Dock, Greenland's £600 million each on the Ram Brewery site and Hertsmere, Dalian Wanda's project at One Nine Elms, Ping An Group's buying up of the Lloyd's building, China Life insurance's purchase of 10 Upper Bank Street, etc.

When changes are happening in a rather short time span and with great speed, it usually brings up a lot of special demands and requirements from the group of people who are affected by these changes.

Mainland Chinese property buyers have been labeled as 'demanding' and sometimes 'difficult' in our property circle. When I met up with my friends in this industry, we usually started with a rather difficult case or a difficult demand or particular behaviour that highlighted our day in a rather challenging way; I could relate to that because not all of my clients are easy either.

But I also sympathise hugely with my clients. I feel as if I can relate to their frustrations and their struggles very closely and dearly.

Whenever I see a couple looking for a property for their children in London as their student pad, I always see my own parents in them, and I remember those sleepless nights my mum endured and the frustrated voice of my dad on the other end of the telephone line. I understand how badly they want to help their children, to provide the best for them, whereas they cannot do that much in a country which they cannot call home, or where they cannot even make their own words understood!

Whenever I see a person who is enthusiastic about investing in London, trying to make the best out of their money and himself/herself, I somehow can see myself in them. The struggle that I had when I was in a similar situation, the silly theory that I had come up with myself in order to overcome my own fear and worries, pretending to be smart while I was not.

I wanted to help and I was trying my best to help any way I could. My we-chat became a question hotline, my phone was ringing even during the weekends, and I started to write articles in Chinese and in English.

I also started to work harder to make myself more professional, more knowledgeable; I started to take up and pass the professional qualifications, I started to give speeches at seminars and events, I started to complete multi-million pound deals, and I started to have clients repeatedly come back to me for more help.

Then I saw one simple fact that we have all overlooked before: the Chinese buyers are difficult and demanding not because they want to be, it is because they don't know how not to be!

If I could make the whole process clearer to them, create a simple system and easy to follow steps, if I could equip them with the knowledge and confidence, if they could have a rather enjoyable, exciting and memorable property-buying experience in the UK like it should be, then the buyers won't be that difficult after all.

So the million dollar questions are: Can I do it? Is this achievable?

The answers are "Yes" and "Yes"!

Let's play a game together. All you need are a pen, a timer and a simple instruction.

See this diagram below? OK, now, circle the numbers in sequence from 1 to 100, you have 1 minute to do this. So you need to circle 1, then find 2, circle it, then find 3, then circle it; you will need to keep doing this until your time is up! Are you with me?

When you are ready, set the timer, and off you go!

	41	81	97	13		58		98		54	
49	1 73		37 5	61	29	2		26	22 10		90
77	33 9	69	57	45	89 21		18	74	38 86	46	62
17			25		93	78 30	50	70 14		34	42
	15			65	53	94	66		82 6		
	7	91		47			52	24		100	16 56
87 11			79		63 99	72	48	88 12	64 4	28	
	67	3	59	35 15	75		8 96		76	20	92 36
95		39	71 55		19 23	44 60		32 68		84	
27	51 83		43	31		80				40	

How many numbers have you managed to circle in these 60 seconds? Was it difficult? The numbers can look quite daunting and all over the place, right?

OK, now try this game again. This time, I am giving you a little hint. See the line I have drawn there? These two lines have divided the picture into four sections. Try to find 1 to 4 now, you will see I have lined up the numbers in order, spreading them equally in these four sections in sequence. Now, set the timer again and see how many numbers you can circle this time.

	41	81	97	13		58		98		54	
49	1 73		37 5	61	29	2		26	22 10		90
77	33	69 9	57	45	89 21		18	74	38 86	46	62
17			25		93	78 30	50	70 14		34	42
	85			65	53	94	66		82 6		
	7	91		47			52	24		100	16 56
87 11			79		63 99	72	48	88 12	64 4	28	
	67	3	59	35 15	75		8 96		76	20	92 36
95		39	71 55		19 23	44 60		32 68		84	
27	51 83		43	31		80					40

Do you find the numbers are now looking clearer to you and the game much easier? I bet you have circled much more numbers than the first time too!

So what made the difference?

It is rather simple and obvious, right? I have told you about the rules that I have used to arrange the numbers in the first place; and then I drew the two lines to make the rules apparent to you. By doing this, I am giving you the power of knowledge and anticipation — your knowledge of the hidden rules of the game will give you the confidence and a good head start compared to those people who do not possess the same knowledge; your acute anticipation of finding one number from one section of this picture in the right sequence makes it possible for you to be more efficient and effective with limited time resources by dividing the scattered information into an organised order.

In this case, knowledge and information turned you into a SMART player. When you play smart, you will play well, when you play well, you will feel more relaxed and at ease, thus the game and the experience of playing the game will become much more enjoyable to you and people that are playing with you.

Buying a property in a foreign country or even buying a property for the first time in your own country, in my eyes, is exactly like the game you have just played.

There are some hidden rules of how this industry works which you can learn and there are some invisible tips that you can follow to simplify your property buying process. Just imagine how your whole experience of buying will be transformed if you have the knowledge and information to know how to buy SMART?!

Have you ever listened to Steve Jobs' speech at Stanford University? One of the things he said was, "You can't connect the dots looking forward; you can only connect them looking backward. So you have to trust that the dots will somehow connect in your future."

As I sit down at my desk on a sunny Monday morning in April 2015 and begin writing this book, I am connecting those dots with great hope that this book will become one of your major dots when you decide to invest in UK properties.

Happy reading and happy UK property buying!

Sally Jing Wang
London

Part One

The Beginning

"A journey of a thousand miles begins
with a single step"

-------- LAO – TZU

Chapter One
It's all about YOU!

Before you meet me or hold this book in your hand, or talk to any other property professionals in this country, your journey of buying a property in the UK probably has already started.

It might have started years ago when you sent your children here for further education and you told yourself that you would buy a property for them so that they have a secured, comfortable place to live, whereas you can also see your money being put to a better place rather than being spent as rent to pay someone else's mortgage; it might have started fairly recently when you saw the news about all those big Chinese companies buying up in London, and you started to see more and more friends around you talking about this or having done this successfully; it might have started from your own childhood, the dream of being able to have a different lifestyle when you were successful, to live in a country that offers different culture, opportunities, history and life style, and now the time is ripe; it might have started a couple of seconds ago when you decided to read this book, with all that is happening in the Chinese stock market at the moment, you are looking for an alternative way of investment ... whatever your reasons are and whenever your journey began, you all share the same goal of this journey – to find the perfect property that is right for you with minimum hassle and the best value.

With this goal in mind, you marched out to an industry and a country that were highly likely to be out of your existing comfort zone, and what did you do? Did you start asking around with lots and lots of questions, sometimes all over the place? Did you constantly worry that you were about to make a really bad decision because you were not sure about a lot of things? Did you go around and talk to quite a few sales people, but were really indecisive about whom to trust? Did you find you had way too much time deciding which one to buy while the property prices just kept going up?

If any of those sound familiar, not to worry, you are not alone! In my own experience of helping a rather large number of international clients, mostly Chinese buyers, I have noticed some patterns that not only apply to you — as the international buyer — but also to some first time local buyers. Below are just two of many:

• Questions! A lot of questions! Questions that cover all areas, all directions! Relevant and irrelevant! The thought and the fact of buying a property in a foreign country, or a first time buyer about to make one of the most expensive purchases in life, turn you into a "question machine"!

"What stocks do you have?"

"How much are they?"

"Where are the good schools?"

"Shall we buy in London?"

"Can I trust you?"

"Is it safe in this area?"

"Do you think it's a good idea to invest in UK properties?"
……..

I don't blame you and I completely understand it! I was probably worse than you when I started! It is overwhelming and you purely don't know where to start.

• Being indecisive. Especially the Chinese clients and the first time buyers that I have met.

"What do you think of this site? Another agent just introduced it to me yesterday and said that I should buy."

"I just put down a reservation fee on this unit yesterday, but my friend said I should keep looking, what do you think?"

"I like this, but maybe there are better ones coming up soon, what do you think?"

Again, I can relate to this; you are worried and you are not sure. After all, this is not your area, you are probably experts in many other fields but this might not be where your strength is! The fact that buying a piece of London or the UK comes with a high price tag, even for the rich, only makes the situation worse.

I have a fantastic deal closing record, but I also hold the water drinking record, from too much talking with the clients, especially the Chinese buyers; and a lot of times I lose my voice towards the end of the viewing day because of all the questions I had to answer.

Don't get me wrong, I am not saying that you should not start this journey by asking questions, those are good questions, questions that you might have been thinking about over and over again, after months, days and nights of discussions with your family, friends and whomever you have bumped into that have bought a property in the UK in the past. After all, to buy a property in a foreign country, especially in one of the most expensive countries in the world, can be daunting! I completely understand that.

But what I want to stress here is that rather than overwhelm yourself and the professionals who are helping you with a large number of random questions, you could make it much more efficient and productive by asking a small quantity of the RIGHT questions.

To be able to do this, you should direct the questions back to yourself first; start from within before you seek answers from outside. At this stage, it should be "it's all about you"!

Property searching in many ways is like soul searching; you need to ask yourself some serious questions and know the answers before you can embark on this journey. I cannot stress how important this is! Without clarity about yourself, you will struggle getting the right message across, obtaining the right help and information, and you will end up with wasted time, energy and undesired results.

So what are the questions that you should ask yourself?

Question 1:
Why do YOU want to buy a property in the UK?

Most of the time, it's the simplest question that makes the biggest difference.

Finding out the real reasons for you to buy a property in the UK will lead you to ask the right questions and look in the right directions. For instance, if your reason is to use the property as an investment, then you know you should focus on questions like the future development plans in the area, rental return, capital gains prediction, past growth rate record, activities of resale or rental in that local market, mortgage repayment etc; if you are buying property as a student pad for your kids, then you should focus on questions like the transportation links, the safety of the area, the local shops, the efficiency of the management team if something goes wrong with the property, etc; if you are buying a self-use residence, then you will be better off asking questions such as: what's the local community like? Are there many good schools around? What's the safety status in that area? What are the surrounding amenities?

Knowing your own reasons will also help you to project yourself as a READY buyer and make the property agents take you more seriously. Yes, you might have all the attention at home; yes, you might have all the respect and social status in your own community from what you have achieved; yes, you might know that you are a good buyer and can act quickly. But without the clarity of knowing the reason behind your search, to the property agents, you are just a shopper who needs a lot of work rather than a HOT lead that deserves their immediate attention.

A couple of years ago, I met this lovely Chinese lady from Shanghai on one of my business trips; after finding out what I do for a living, she said, "Sally, can you help me look for a property in the UK? I have been looking around for about a year and I still have many questions, but a lot of agents that I spoke to before don't reply to my emails or we-chat anymore, instead, they just keep sending me the property details. I am so annoyed as most of them are not what I want!" Her frustration was so profound that I can still remember her facil expression and the question she repeatedly asked me: "I have money, I am a cash buyer, why don't those agents take me seriously and why can't I find the property I need to buy?!"

Well, I bet those agents had been taking her pretty seriously at the beginning, but after endless aimless research and question-answer marathon sessions, most of them will naturally have grown tired of running around like a headless chicken and consider her a less desirable "shopper" who requires a lot of time and work. As a result, they simply put her on their general mailing list. Sales agents anywhere in the world live on commissions and they are trained to tell the difference between a hot immediate lead and a cold long-term lead, and they have developed their own system of treating different levels of leads with different levels of attention. For you to be able to buy smart, you need to build up a solid close professional relationship with a good property agent to keep you on top of the trend in the UK property market and provide you with the first hand reliable information.

Knowing your reasons for buying will also greatly reduce the search load and narrow down the options, sooner. There are hundreds of thousands of properties on the market for sale at any point in the UK, only by knowing what you want from this purchase can you work towards the right direction sooner.

Question 2:
What is YOUR budget?

Money has never been an easy topic.

A lot of my clients in the past thought I was rude and nosy by asking them this question at our first meeting. After all, not every wealthy person wants the world to know they have money, certainly not a woman that they just met. I cannot tell you how many times I got answers like this: "Sally, we don't have a budget. See what you can find for us."

Unfortunately, "no budget" often leads to "no right property" for "a long time". After all, this is one of the most important references we are using in the UK property market! Without this, you are really looking for a needle in a haystack.

So how do you work out your budget?

Firstly, you need to decide whether this is a cash purchase or if you will need to use a mortgage. If you are a cash buyer, easy peasy, whatever you want to put down will be your budget, just bear in mind some extra costs such as stamp duty, solicitor fee, etc. I will cover this in a separate chapter soon.

Secondly, if this involves a mortgage, then you need to find out how much you can borrow. As an international property buyer, you can either speak to a broker or the bank directly, depending on which country you are coming from. For our Chinese buyers, Bank of China offers mortgage services, so you can start talking to them. However, do remember that not everyone can give you financial advice; most agents are not able to help you. In the UK, one needs to be qualified and regulated by a financial institution to be able to give financial advice. So, do not take advice from anyone and everyone just because they said you should listen to them!

Thirdly, give yourself some breaking room on the budget. Although there are times you will be able to get a discount, this is not guaranteed to happen every single time. In the past, I have managed to get a 10% discount for an apartment worth just under 4 million pounds; but I have also come across situations in which my clients are considered to be lucky just to get a plot in a site that was extremely popular. You should always bear in mind the extra costs and prepare for the worst. Give yourself some space to breathe, you will find yourself much more relaxed. After all, there is no need to stress yourself out and this is one way to avoid it from the very beginning.

Question 3:
What's YOUR timeline?

Your timeline for the property will help decide what type of properties you should be focusing on in the property search stage.

If you need the property NOW, then you need to concentrate on the second hand market, as those are the ready stocks. However, you still need to pay attention to terms like "AST" — assured short-hold tenancy, which means there is a tenancy agreement currently in place for the property; you need to find out when the tenancy will be ending to see whether that suits your timeline.

You will also need to pay attention to terms like "chain", which is an expression to indicate whether the seller of the property needs to find a place to buy before they can complete the transaction of selling their property to you. In an ideal circumstance, you want to find a property that "has no chain" to avoid the possibility of the deal falling though or unexpected waiting time. If the seller cannot find a property to buy and to move to, they might decide not to sell their current property. To us property professionals, it means the chain is broken; to you, it means you will lose all the money that you have spent up to that point and you need to start the whole searching process all over again.

If you are not in desperate need of the property and can wait for a few months to a year or two, then the new development market will be your best bet.

This is the piece of information that our Chinese buyers haven't registered in their mind just yet! I have received so many requests in the past: "Sally, find us a brand new property. I need to use it in a couple of months' time, and can we view the property soon, let's say tomorrow, before I go back to China this weekend?"

The Chinese culture and the desire to have minimum hassle in the future has led to the majority of Chinese buyers at this stage requiring brand new properties. However, the reality is that the majority of developers in the UK tend to start selling right after they secure the land deal and planning permission. In London, with reputable developers, sometimes we are talking about a couple of years before the completion date.

Which means, yes, you can BUY a brand new apartment NOW, but you cannot HAVE it NOW. Yes, you can visit the site NOW, but most likely what you'll see is only a hole in the ground and if you are lucky, you might be able to visit the sales and marketing suite to see the show apartment if one is available.

Saying this does not mean it is absolutely impossible for you to buy a brand new property that you can use shortly after the completion. You can still make it if you are open to re-assigned units or if you are looking at luxury family homes. "Re-assigned units" means that the buyer who purchased the new build apartment/house decides to sell it on before the completion date, the price of this will usually be lower than the market price from the developers at the point of selling. If you do this right, you can certainly bag a bargain. However, this type of transaction requires you to have a rather large amount of cash ready and it does involve a lot of different complications; you have to make sure your agent or you know exactly what you are doing.

The other possible situation is if you are looking at buying a luxury expensive property or a penthouse. Those types of properties are not for the mass market; they are waiting for the right type of buyers to come along, which means it takes time for them to be sold. Some developers won't even start marketing those types of properties before they are built purely because their high profile clients prefer to see the finished product before they make a decision.

Sometimes, other people's misfortune can lead to your lucky buy as well. Once I managed to secure a brand new show-house for a Chinese family to move in straight away — a beautiful £2.6 million family house in Surrey. The previous buyers had to pull out of the deal due to a sudden change in their financial situation.

Other than that, to buy a brand new apartment in London with immediate usage is pretty much mission-impossible.

Question 4:
What's YOUR travelling arrangement?

Do you need a visa to come to the UK? Is it in place? How long can you stay in the UK each time? And how fast can you get on that plane if needed? These are the questions you need to ask yourself before you consider buying a property in the UK.

A lot of experienced property investors have passed the stage of seeing the property itself before they can make the decision; a large number of Hong Kong, Macao and Singapore buyers are able to do this, partially because they have deeply rooted relationships with the UK, partially because frequent exhibitions are held almost every weekend at their doorstep.

For mainland Chinese buyers, the story is different. When I left China 14 years ago to pursue my further education in the UK, the number of Chinese people in the UK was limited, the travelling restrictions were still in place and people's knowledge of the UK was very little. 14 years later, we have more and more Chinese buying properties in the UK, especially in the past 2-3 years; there is more and more media coverage on the UK property market especially with Wanda's, Greenland's and ABP's activities in London, more and more social media platforms have been established to bridge this gap between the UK property market and the Chinese consumer groups.

But these are not enough. To be able to have the confidence to put down the money on a property here in UK, these buyers still need to fly over, sometimes to see the site, to get a feel for the neighbourhood, to meet the agent, to get the documents done, etc. Mainland Chinese buyers are not there yet! There are so many times when a good new development came to my desk and my mainland Chinese buyers were still struggling to decide on whether to buy or not, while my Hong Kong clients had already started to work on the floor plans and snatched up the best units in the block.

If this is the case for you, then you need to ensure that you have all the related travelling arrangements in place. Because if the right property comes up and you need to see it to be able to make the decision, my advice to you would be — get on that plane as soon as possible, to reduce the risk of that property being snatched up by others who can make that decision without seeing the property.

Question 5:
How well do YOU know the UK?

This is a tough question in a sense; as much as you would like to say that you know a lot about everything, as much as you want to show your agent that you are an experienced buyer (in order to minimise the risk that they will use this against you and sell you some rubbish stocks because of your limited knowledge), you need to be absolutely honest with yourself on this one.

Do you know the UK well? Do you know the UK property market well? Do you have property buying experience in an overseas market, not necessarily in the UK? Are you confident that the knowledge you possess about the UK is from reliable sources? Because you will need to make decisions based on the knowledge that you currently possess.

If your knowledge about the UK is pretty good, then congratulations! Believe it or not, you are well ahead a lot of other people. I have worked with a number of Chinese buyers that do not even know how to use a London tube map or what "postcode" or "zone" mean. If you think your knowledge about the UK is just as bad, do not worry. You do not need to share this with everyone, this book will teach you how to still buy smart by asking the right questions, doing the right research yourself with minimum time and effort, while keeping your ears open to the advice and opinions of professionals who are the best group of people that can feel the pulse of the property industry here in the UK. But before that, you need to be 100% honest with yourself so you know where you stand in this game.

Question 6:
What's YOUR biggest concern?

I always ask my clients to tell me their biggest concern from the very beginning. To me, I believe that everyone deserves to know exactly what he or she is getting into before they start the journey. No one likes nasty surprises, especially with this amount of time, money and emotional commitment.

Hence, it is absolutely necessary for you to write down the biggest concern that you have so that you can look for answers from the very beginning before any commitment.

Below are some examples of my clients' biggest concerns:

"My daughter insists on buying a property in London as she doesn't want to rent any more, however, she is on a work permit; if we buy a property for her now, what if three years later, the work permit doesn't work out, and she needs to come back to China? What will happen to the property? Can we sell it? How do we get the money back to China as none of us are there at that time?" (This was also my mum's biggest concern when I decided to go for my first purchase years ago.)

"I am paying for an off-plan new apartment now, what if in two years' time, upon completion, I move in and find there are big structural problems to the property, like the roof is leaking, what do I do? The show flat looks good, but what if the quality of the finished product is nothing like the show flat?"

"Let's say that I buy this off-plan new apartment from an agent now and use a law firm to carry out the legal documents; what if shortly afterwards, the agent or the law firm goes bankrupt; what will happen to my property? As it will not be complete in a couple of years' time?"

"I have found the perfect property, and have everything ready to go, what if the deal falls through, what do I do?"

"I am going to buy a second-hand property. How do I know by the time the solicitors tell me that the deal has completed, the house is mine? I don't speak the language, don't read the language; how do I know the solicitors did transfer the ownership?"

To buy a property in your own country is already stressful, let alone to buy a property in a foreign country! I know those are the questions that keep my clients up at night, worrying about things that are happening on the other side of the world with time differences and language barriers.

Every one of you deserves to clarify these concerns before you take your next move.

Ask yourself what YOUR biggest concerns are and look for the answers.

QUESTION 7:
Do YOU have a location in mind?

Let's face it; although the UK is much smaller geographically than China, it is still very hard to know where to buy if you don't know that much about it. Every city has its streets and neighbourhoods that are considered to be better than others, and every city has its hot spots that are attracting more government funding, and are considered to be upcoming areas with more chances to do better for your investment in the future.

So, do you already have a location in mind? If your answer to this is yes, what are your reasons for choosing this location? Are your reasons from your friends and family? From information you found on a website? Or from your own experience in the past? Are you confident that your choice of location is the best at the time you are making the decision? How much do you know about the changes that are about to happen in the location you have chosen? How much do you know about the local people's opinion on this location that you have chosen? Those are just a few questions that you need to ask in order to put your choice of location to the test. This book will teach you how to do that.

If you don't have a location in mind, not to worry, you are not alone; the majority of my Chinese clients do not know where to buy when they come to me, but with the right amount of guidance, you will be on the right track in no time.

In the past years, I have come up with a simple system called RAQ: Do your Research, find the Agent you can trust and ask the right Questions. In the following chapters, I will show you what to research and how to do it, how you know you have found the right agent, and the right questions to ask.

Once you have found yourself the right person to work with, have equipped yourself with the right knowledge from research and know the right questions to ask, in other words, when you can BUY SMART, you will find the whole experience of finding a property in the UK a much more enjoyable experience than you thought.

QUESTION 8:
How much can YOU afford to lose?

When I entered the property industry, one of the first lessons that my mentor taught me was, "Don't think about how much money you can make! Think about how much you can afford to lose." During the years, I have grown to learn the real meaning behind this piece of wisdom.

Buying properties can be very impulsive and addictive, especially when you have done well in the past, or if you haven't got the experience but suddenly find yourself being thrown into a rather heated situation and need to make a quick decision. To know how much you can afford to lose will help you to stay calm and make the right choice that is suitable to your circumstances rather than make impulsive moves.

In the past years I have witnessed people who bought dozens of units at a time and then went bankrupt when the economy took an unpleasant downturn against their favour; they acted too ambitiously because they misjudged their affordability of losing. I have also witnessed people missing out on great buying opportunities right in front of their eyes. Then, the market took off because the supply kept falling while the demand kept growing. They acted too passively and indecisively because they were not sure how much they could afford to lose.

After all, this is a "game" that comes with its own risks.

"A journey of a thousand miles begins with a single step." The first single step you should take on this journey is asking yourself these eight questions! Once you have all the answers, then good news: you are ready to move on to the next stage...

It's all about YOU questionnaire

Question One:
Why do YOU want to buy a property in the UK?

Question Two:
How much is YOUR budget?

Question Three:
What's YOUR time line?

Question Four:
What's YOUR travelling arrangement?

Question Five:
How well do YOU know the UK?

Question Six:
What is YOUR biggest concern?

Question Seven:
Do YOU have a location in mind?

Question Eight:
How much can YOU afford to lose?

Chapter Two
It's All About the "Property" Too!

To me, finding the right property is also like finding the right partner. First of all, you need to find out who you are and what your own needs are, then you need to get to know and try to understand your potential partner: Who are they? What do they want? What are their characteristics, strengths and weaknesses, etc.? The more you know, the easier it is for you to know whether that person is "THE ONE" for you or not.

If you have done your question and answer exercise from chapter one, then now it is time for you to gain some knowledge and understanding of the other party — "UK properties".

When people think about UK properties, they tend to think of certain things. They think of the cost, they think of the leases, they think of return, they think of English gardens... But when I think of UK properties, I think about "people", "human beings", "individuals". To me, each property is just like us human beings, they have their own age, style, structure, unique character, their own weaknesses and strengths.

Some of them are old, very old with history; others are young, vibrant and full of modern technology; some of them require little attention; others are very high maintenance; some of them appeared to be very nice at the beginning, but will shock you with all the scary skeletons in the closet; others keep impressing you with their reliability and the persistent ability to deliver, although they appeared very simple and bland at the beginning.

To be able to make the right decision for you, you need to at least have a basic understanding of the stereotypes of properties here in the UK and then put some heart into it, rather than just considering them as stone and concrete. If you don't like the property yourself and the thought of living there put you off strongly, the chances are your next buyer or your future tenants will probably feel the same!

Here I'd like to share a story with you. A client had purchased an apartment near Battersea Power Station about a decade ago.

"What a fantastic investment!" you would say, especially with everything that is happening now in that part of London. "They must have made a fortune!"

Yes, they would have if they still had that property. The reality is that they sold it shortly after they bought it.

"Why?" you would ask, and that is exactly the same question that I asked them. Let's just assume that they did not foresee the future of the area at that point of time; the simple fact of re-selling a unit shortly after purchasing it without making any money puzzled me.

Then, their answers made me understand where the problems were. When they were buying at that time, they got their numbers wrong: they stretched their budget to the top limit and they failed to register the piece of information about the service charge;

coupled with the fact that they suffered a few months of not having a tenant in the flat to cover their mortgage payment, they decided that unit was not for them and they chose to sell it on. Although this is a result caused by a chain of events, if they had a solid idea about the property and what comes with each property type, they would have been more prepared financially and avoided the costly mistake of getting the numbers wrong in the first place. And yes, with all that is happening now in Battersea, they could have made a fortune if they had kept that unit.

So what are the basic things you need to at least have some understanding and knowledge of about UK properties?

Start with my "SAT" system: Style, Age and Type, and follow up with looking at the details.

"SAT"
– STYLE

All houses were designed and built by people. People lived through different historical eras with the changes in working patterns, social responsibilities, population, wealth, class and technology , etc. As a result, the houses' styles are a reflection of the change of a society and the needs of the people at the time they were built.

This is particularly true in the UK. Here, I am only going to share the most typical types of property for that period.

Around 1714 – 1830: Georgian Period

To me, those hundred or so years have produced some of the most beautiful and grand houses in the UK.

Most of them were typically large three and four storey terraces with vertical sliding (sash) windows glazed with small panels, classical symmetrical design, very decorative features around the windows, doors and ironwork, high quality brick walls, usually painted white with timber floors, ornate and grand interior design.

1837 - 1901: Victorian Period

This was the period of industrial revolution when there was a large movement of the rural population to towns and cities. An urgent demand was created for cheap housing on a large scale to accommodate the workers. Those houses tend to be terraced houses with back yards and alleys connected together with the neighbours. The floor plan will typically have two small living rooms, a kitchen or scullery downstairs, two or perhaps three small bedrooms upstairs with no bathroom anywhere inside the house originally. The toilet would normally be outside.

However, these have since been modernised to include internal bathrooms and WCs.

1901 - 1918: Edwardian Period

Edwardian style housing reflected the UK's prosperity before the First World War. These large houses were built on the outskirts of major towns and cities, as they then existed. Now, they may be considered to be inner city locations. They originally housed the professional classes and their servants.

With Edwardian style properties, you will be expecting to see large bay windows, decorative brickwork and stonework, front and back gardens, cavity walls, large rooms with high ceilings, decorative timber staircases, etc.

1918 – 1939: Inter-war Period

Those twenty-something years saw two styles of properties to meet the huge demand for new houses as a result of the First World War.

In the 1920s, for those who could not afford to buy a house, council house building programs began. These houses usually had brick cavity walls and tile or slate roofs, small front and back gardens, reasonable sized rooms and were often constructed to good standards in short terraces.

In the 1930s, in order to meet the demands for a growing number of wealthy people's need to purchase their own properties, a better class and style of houses were introduced with key features like added damp-proof courses to cavity walls, large bay windows, stone or rendered front faces, bathrooms with toilets and decorative gables.

1945-1970: Post War

The UK was not in a good shape after 1945 and the Second World War; there was a great shortage of materials and skills. As a result, there were not many new houses built between 1945 and 1960. With the growing population and need for new housing, the 1960s saw the creation of large housing estates, with a mix of semi-detached housing, bungalows, and terraced housing of just one or two styles repeated shown on any one housing estate.

Some typical characteristics for these houses are large timber or metal-framed windows, installation of some central heating systems, but still including open fireplaces, and the introduction of timber or plastic facings, garages and gardens for the better properties, etc.

1970 to the present day

There are possibly two big style differences for the properties that were built after the 1970s. One is that they will have a variety in style, house type and size so that each property looks unique when developers plan estates; the other is that there are many traits of the home built to be energy efficient, such as small windows, double glazing, thermal insulation and central heating systems replacing chimneys.

Understanding the styles of the properties not only will make you appear more confident and experienced in front of the agents, but also it helps you to have a much better idea of what you are buying into. Victorian style of properties have more chances to offer you original features such as fireplaces and sash windows, but might have the downsides of producing a higher gas bill in the winter time and being more prone to damp issues; new-built can offer you a more secured car park, concierge services and lower heating bills, but might have the downsides of higher monthly maintenance costs and the lack of the character that you might be looking for.

"SAT"
– AGE

When you are dating someone, wouldn't you want to know how old he or she is? Most of us tend to obtain this piece of information without us even noticing it; we have formed the habit of checking this out unconsciously as part of our human nature. So why are we so interested in knowing the other person's age? Well, this could mean a lot of different things to different people, but fundamentally, age is a very important reference for us to figure out a lot of hidden information about the other person.

If the person sitting opposite you is 100 years old now, that means he/she has a history and a lot of experience such as war, marriage, children (maybe), but also means medical expenses (highly likely), low energy , etc.

If the person sitting opposite you is 20 years old, you know pretty well what kind of things that person will be talking about or interested in; in most of the cases, that individual will have a lot of ambitions, energy and ideas, etc.

So when you are buying a property, why do you want to know how old the property is? When it was built?

This piece of information is far more important than a lot of you initially thought. It can also reveal a lot of hidden information.

For instance, did you know that if a house was built in the 1960s, there is a chance for it to be an old timber framed house? Do you know that if this were the case, you might have trouble obtaining a mortgage?

Did you know that if a flat was built in the 1950s, it might have its lease running less than 100 years if it was a short lease at the beginning? Did you know if this were the case, you would possibly be facing a large cost to renew the lease if you choose to buy it?

Do you know that the age of an off-plan new build property is a good indication as to whether the building insurance and warranty that came with it upon completion is still available by the time you become the new owner? For instance, let's say you bought a new flat which was built 9 years ago with 10 years NHBC warranty to it initially, do you know that you will only have one year free building warranty left after you purchase it?

The general rule is that the more you know about the age of the property, the more you know about the property itself and the more you know where you stand.

"SAT"
– TYPE

The purpose of understanding the type of properties is not only to help you with the understanding of the legal terms that come with the property such as leasehold, freehold, etc., but also to give you a good price indication.

The most commonly used terms for property types in the UK are: detached house, semi-detached house, terraced house, mews house, cottage, bungalow, flat or apartment, conversion flats and maisonette.

Detached house:
A house that has its own grounds and does not share any wall with neighbours.

Semi-detached house:
Houses that are built in pairs, with the individual house being usually one half of the building.

Terraced house:
This is a term for houses that are located in a row on streets with identical or mirror image and shared sidewalls. This type of house is very common throughout the UK.

Mews house:
It has been considered as another term for terraced housing. It may sound more upmarket but in some parts it is reserved for older period properties, often linked to larger detached properties.

Cottage:
To a lot of people, cottage represents English country life, with low ceilings and a front garden full of English roses and summer flowers. Theoretically, the term "cottage" is another word substituted for a terraced house in some parts. It may signify something old and quaint, or may imply a semi-rural or rural location. Again, it may be used because it "sounds" more upmarket.

Bungalows:
This term is usually reserved for a single-storey residential property; such properties can be detached or semi-detached and occasionally in a terrace. If an additional space has been created within the roof void, either by subsequent alteration or by design at the building stage, they will be called something like "dormer bungalows" or "chalet bungalows" depending on the exact style or the part of the country in which they are located. Traditionally, this type of property was occupied by aged population due to the fact that it does not have stairs in the house, however they have gained growing popularity among the younger people nowadays.

Flat:
This is a term that will confuse you a lot, especially if you are also interested in the second hand property market.

In the new development category, flats or apartments should be very familiar to you, regardless of which country you are coming from; you will probably get the idea. However, here in the UK, you will come across terms like "Victorian conversion", "Georgian conversion" and "maisonette". Conversion simply means that people before you have already converted the Victorian or Georgian HOUSE into a number of FLATS. In most parts of the UK, if there are separate external individual entrances to units (such as there are external walkways from external staircases), they will be categorised as "maisonettes".

Now, if these properties were human beings, after obtaining a good understanding of their age, style and type, don't you find suddenly that they are not strangers to you anymore? You now know quite a bit about them, right?

What's even better is that this knowledge will also empower you by giving you some understanding of things that you probably would find rather difficult otherwise.

Legal ownership is one of them. Legal terms have always been considered one of the most boring parts of the business as well as the most difficult, with the legal jargon that we do not use on the daily basis. What if I told you the rule of the legal ownership in the UK is actually very simple and straightforward? And with your "SAT" knowledge, you will be able to guess the majority of the legal ownerships on a property pretty easily.

According to Law of Property Act 1925, the two legal estates in UK are named freehold and leasehold respectively. Generally speaking, houses are freehold and flats are leasehold. In legal terms, freehold is known as "fee simple absolute in possession" and leasehold is known as "a term of years absolute".

In simple English, freehold means that in theory the owner can do anything they like with their property and the land the property is on. (Although in reality, the UK parliament can restrict your right, and your right can have a reasonable limit.)

Leasehold on the other hand means that the owners have exclusive possession of the property for a fixed duration but cannot do anything they like. They own the right to use the property but do not own the land. Their right is limited compare to freehold. And the owner of the leasehold needs to pay for ground rent and service charge. So, the next time your agent tells you that the property you are looking at has a lease on it, you will know what that means.

Ideally, when you purchase a property, you want to have a long lease on it, otherwise not only you will encounter problems with the bank when you want to get a mortgage on it, but also you will be facing the possibility of a large lease renewal fee and a long period of time in getting the lease renewed. Normally, I won't advise my clients to look at properties that have a lease shorter than 100 years, a lot of times shorter than 120 years even, based on their personal situation, unless the property has a good price tag on it in a very favourable area.

So, now you know one of the many good questions to ask the next time you are looking for a property! And you know that when someone tells you "this property has a nice 'long' lease of 70 years", you know what that really means. Although a 70 years lease is considered to be quite long in some parts of the world, such as China, it is certainly not the case here in the UK.

Well, now, as much as both you and I hate to categorise things using money as a reference, we all tend to do that in real life, right? When you go on a blind date and sit in front of a group of people with different jobs, most likely you have a good idea of who earns more and who earns less, right? You usually won't expect a young graduate in a trainee position to earn more than a barrister with 20 years' experience, right?

For us human beings, unfortunately, what we do for a living often reveals to other people of how much we are making.

Same here for the UK properties: knowing the types of properties will also give you some references in understanding the price. Generally speaking, given the other criteria is the same (such as same location, same age, etc.), different types of properties bear a different price (from high to low).

Detached bungalow
Detached house
Semi-detached bungalow
Semi-detached house
Terraced house
Flat

However the sequence might be different if we include the new-build developments.

The Devil is in the detail

Phew! That was a lot! But remember, it was actually not that much; all you need to do is to register your brain with the information above so that when you are choosing the agent to help you with finding the best property, you know what questions to ask and you know whether that agent knows what she or he is talking about.

Now, the things that really need your work and participation are in understanding the details and knowing what to look for, where to look and how to look, especially when you need to make a decision among the shortlisted properties.

How many of you have been given a price list, a floor plan and a site plan of a development and were told that you need to choose the one that you will put your money on?

Many of my clients, especially the not so experienced ones, will become very overwhelmed by this stage. What's worst for them is that the floor plans and site plans are mostly in English. The developers and agents probably can translate the fact sheets, price list and brochures into Chinese, but not all of the floor plans.

So what to do with pages of floor plans, in a language that you do not even understand, but you HAVE to choose that ONE unit you need to buy? (Well, even if you can afford to buy 10, out of a larger number of units available, it is still not that easy.)

My suggestions are to go with what you can understand and use experts' opinions. It's true that you don't understand the language, but you surely will understand the figures and shapes of arrows and pictures. With these three, you will be able to know the size of the property, the facing of it, and also the layout of each room.

Together with your agent's advice, you should be able to make a pretty sound decision in a short period of time. I tend to give my clients the three best options that I like personally for them to choose from. And most of the time, this strategy works out well. By doing so, we will have a better chance to choose good units that fit the clients' requirements.

Square footage is the most popular reference for the size of property here in the UK, whereas in China, people are most accustomed to square meters. 100 square feet is equal to 9.29 square meters. To get a rough idea, for a flat that is around 800 square feet, it will be around 74 square meters, so for a quick calculation, you can wipe off the 0 at the end and reduce the first number by 1. For instance if you were told the flat is around 920 square feet, you take away that 0 at the end, make it 92, and then deduct 9 by 1, which give you the number of 82 square meters. (The true figure is 85 square meters or so.)

You see, pretty close but much simpler, compared to having to use your calculator and multiple 920 by 0.0929. (1 square foot is equal to 0.0929 square meters.)

The good news is that the size of a flat here in the UK generally refers to the internal size ONLY and it refers to the actual space that can be used, not the structural size, unlike in China. So "what you see is what you get"!

Next, what you need to look at on the floor plan is the facing; normally it is shown with an arrow pointing north to give you a reference. Once you understand this, then you will have a pretty good idea of what the natural light in the property is going to be like and what the views from inside of the property are.

If you are looking at buying a completed or second hand property, then there is one extra thing you need to be able to understand, which is the EPC (short for Energy Performance Certificate). In most of the cases, by law, you MUST be shown an Energy Performance certificate for FREE before buying the property (in most of the cases).

An EPC looks like this: (From www.gov.uk)

Energy Performance Certificate (EPC)

17 Any Street, District, Any Town, B5 5XX

Dwelling type: Detached house	**Reference number:** 0919-9628-8430-2785-5996
Date of assessment: 15 August 2011	**Type of assessment:** RdSAP, existing dwelling
Date of certificate: 13 March 2012	**Total floor area:** 165 m²

Use this document to:

- Compare current ratings of properties to see which properties are more energy efficient
- Find out how you can save energy and money by installing improvement measures

Estimated energy costs of dwelling for 3 years	£5,367
Over 3 years you could save	£2,865

Estimated energy costs of this home

	Current costs	Potential costs	Potential future savings
Lighting	£375 over 3 years	£207 over 3 years	
Heating	£4,443 over 3 years	£2,073 over 3 years	You could save £2,865 over 3 years
Hot water	£549 over 3 years	£222 over 3 years	
Totals:	**£5,367**	**£2,502**	

These figures show how much the average household would spend in this property for heating, lighting and hot water. This excludes energy use for running appliances like TVs, computers and cookers, and any electricity generated by microgeneration.

Energy Efficiency Rating

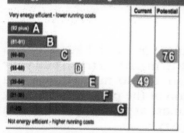

The graph shows the current energy efficiency of your home.

The higher the rating the lower your fuel bills are likely to be.

The potential rating shows the effect of undertaking the recommendations on page 3.

The average energy efficiency rating for a dwelling in England and Wales is band D (rating 60).

Top actions you can take to save money and make your home more efficient

Recommended measures	Indicative cost	Typical savings over 3 years	Available with Green Deal
1 Increase loft insulation to 270 mm	£100 - £350	£141	✓
2 Cavity wall insulation	£500 - £1,500	£537	✓
3 Draught proofing	£80 - £120	£78	✓

See page 3 for a full list of recommendations for this property.

To find out more about the recommended measures and other actions you could take today to save money, visit **www.direct.gov.uk/savingenergy** or call **0300 123 1234** (standard national rate). When the Green Deal launches, it may allow you to make your home warmer and cheaper to run at no up-front cost.

Page 1 of 4

What you need to pay attention to is this bar in particular (see below picture), which gives you a grading on a scale of A-G via a graph coloured from green through yellow and orange to red. A is the best and G the worst. Numerically the scale is from 1-100 with 100 being the best and 0 the worst.

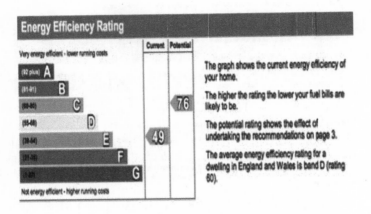

Even writing this makes me feel like it is too technical and this is going to make you try to pull your hair out again, given there are so many things you need to think about on top of the pressure of buying a property — one of the most expensive purchases in your life in a foreign country.

Not to worry: all you need to do is to familiarise yourself with the look of this graph and know this will be one of the questions that you might need to ask when purchasing a completed property or a second hand one. Go with common sense on this one — you want the efficiency level to be high, as this will also affect the price of the property.

The last is always the best, and I have saved the most difficult but most useful piece of information till the end. "Look at the details of the real property with the knowledge that you have on property structure and look for signs of problems."

A lot of my clients, especially the buyers with some experience, think this is unnecessary; after all, we are not trained and qualified to be surveyors, why do we need to do this? Why not leave it to the professionals? It took them years of studying to get their qualification, how possible is this for us to learn in such a short period of time?

Let me set up a scenario for you here. Let us imagine that you are going on a blind date with a man/woman that you have not met before, but were given a brief summary of him/her in advance. When sitting down opposite that person, you notice that he/she has a mark of wedding ring on his/her hand, ten minutes into the conversation you notice that he/she has been telling you stories that do not make sense and contradict each other. So what are your reactions? The mark of the wedding ring might be an indication of him/her lying to you about his/her marriage status; you would of course suspect that he/she took the ring off right before he/she came to see you. His/her contradicting stories might be a sign of his/her habit and ability to lie. Would you still go out with him/her? The chances are pretty slight here unless you have a really good reason.

The same with property, if you know what signs to look for, then you know what the fundamental deal breaker will be for you. For instance, if you don't want to spend huge amounts of money to fix up the structural problems of the property, when you see cracks near the ground, when you see something is missing from the roof, when you see cracks from the ceiling downwards on the second floor, especially in an end-of-terrace, the chances of you making the deal will be next to zero. Otherwise, you will be possibly looking at fixing the foundations, the roof , etc.

But those can only be picked out when you train your brain where to look and what to look for. Again, if you are not sure, find an experienced agent that you can trust and seek professional advice and guidance.

To be able to identify problems like this at a very early stage before you put down an offer and start the legal process will save you money (on a solicitor, surveyor , etc.) and also will save you the energy, time and most importantly your emotional disappointment.

The key places to look at (especially when you are interested in second hand properties) are foundations, floors, walls and roofs.

The key problems that you should be looking for are foundation failure, movements in walls, roof problems and dampness issues (especially dry rot fungus).

One final note: if you've read this far, I want to compliment you because, unfortunately, you're in the top 10% of people who bought a non-fiction book and read past the first chapter. That's right, this was backed up statistically. How insane is that? The reason for me to start writing this book was because there was no book like this for Chinese buyers at the moment and my Chinese clients have asked me, time and time again, a lot of random questions. I wanted to help and provide something simple but also give you the opportunity to go deeper!

So before you turn the page, let me quickly highlight some of the questions that will make you look confident and knowledgeable for the products you are about to buy – UK properties.

It's all about "THE PROPERTY" Questions

Questions around the "SAT":
style, age and type of the property

What's the legal ownership on the property?

How many years on the lease for this property
(if it's leasehold)?

What's your recommendation of the units that I
should choose from? And why?
(when choosing a unit base on the floor plan)

Can I have a copy of the EPC?
(for completed or second hand property)

And remember — also look for the signs of potential problems.

See, it's not as difficult as you would have thought, is it?! Once you understand the concept, you will find it actually quite a fun and educational process.

After all, a successful property investment is like a fabulous relationship; you stay because you are having a great time!

Chapter Three
Location! Location! Location!

In property circles, we have a common saying about the three most important factors in property market appraisal – Location! Location! Location! If you compare similar types of properties in different areas, you will discover significant variations in prices, whether they are new homes or second hand units. In London, you will be looking at significant price differences for similar types of properties even on streets that are pretty close to each other in the same area.

Hence, I cannot stress enough the importance of getting the location right, and more importantly, RIGHT for YOU.

Now, picture this: you have decided to buy a property in the UK, you have all the answers to the questions in chapter one, you have a basic idea of what was covered in chapter two about the UK properties. You look at a UK map and you get stuck.

"Where shall I start the search?" you would ask yourself. Compared to many countries, especially China, the UK is not that big, but it is still big enough for you to feel lost in front of the map, especially when you don't speak the language.

You may go out and ask around in order to get ideas of where will be your best bet. Perhaps colleagues who have visited the UK in the past? Maybe your family friends who have bought a property or two in the UK? Maybe some agents based in your city that are selling UK properties, or maybe even your children who you've sent to the UK to study a couple of years ago...

You probably don't need me to go through each one of them to tell you what ingredient will be missing from the above options... Yes, your colleagues have visited the UK once or even many times, but the places they visited either are tourism spots or work related; yes, your family friends have bought a property or two in the UK, but that was based on THEIR requirements and needs, not YOURS – they might prefer to stay on a busy road but you prefer to be in a quite location, they might have bought their place for their son to stay while he is studying his undergraduate course in LSE, but your oldest daughter is only 12 in a private school in Surrey; yes, you might have talked to a few agents in your city, but you might have also noticed that not all of them have even visited the UK and at probably half of your age, will you be confident enough to trust them? Yes, your children have been in London for the past two years and have travelled a lot, eaten at a lot of places and been on a few cultural field trips, but are they able to provide you with the knowledge that you need in order to make a sound financial decision?

What will make it worse is that when you talk to real professionals who can be of help to you, you will find a lot of information they are trying to get across to you is very difficult to understand. For instance, let's say an agent sends you a good development in London and suggests you buy: "You should buy this, it is in Zone 1, East London and it is even on the north of the river, with this price! It's a bargain, you should go for it."

Will you be able to really understand this message?

If you don't have a professional to work closely with on your search, you probably will find yourself struggling more every time a new agent registers your details and asks, "How much is your budget? And where are you looking?" If you don't even know what the options for "where" are, how will you be able to give the right answer? You cannot simply tell them that your location is anywhere in the UK, right?

Well, the good news is that you can save years of time, tons of travelling — and in a few minutes — by simply following these steps.

The property industry often tries to make our field feel incredibly complex. Well, it is to some extent, but in reality, once you get past the jargon and the references that we are using in the UK, it's relatively simple.

Step One: Get the big picture

Take out the UK map that you have, or find one on the internet; I am going to use the following map for demonstration purposes.

I am pretty sure that you are very familiar with this image, and I believe that it will be quite easy for you to decide where to go among the choices of Scotland, England, Wales and Northern Ireland at this early stage. Currently, the majority of Chinese buyers are locating themselves in England, with a small amount in the other parts unless they have their own personal reasons, which could be either that their children are studying there or they have a business running there.

Then you can break the map down to major cities. To my Chinese clients who have no idea where to invest in, a good starting point to narrow down the options is deciding between these two categories: London or other university towns. If you have a good amount of money, London might be on the top of your list; but if not, other university towns also have the potential to deliver a good performance with a lower cost.

So, back to chapter one: ask yourself those eight questions, then you will be able to narrow down your starting point in no time.

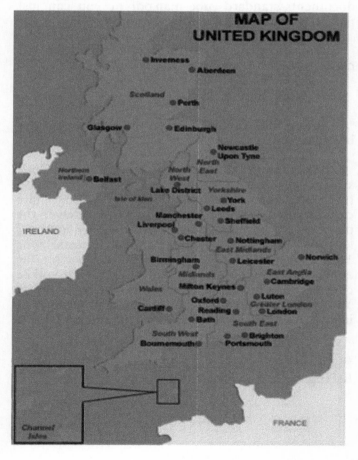

Step Two: Make the London tube map your best friend and get familiar with terms like "zone", "postcode", "south or north of the river", "west or east", "boroughs" and some specific names for some areas.

The first thing I always give to my clients, whether I am at an exhibition in the Far East or meeting the clients for the first time in the UK, is a "London Tube map". Trust me, make it your best friend and you will feel like a pro within days. (You can download a version here https://www.tfl.gov.uk/cdn/static/cms/documents/standard-tube-map.pdf or you can just pick it up at any London tube station.)

And I am going to go through some of the key characteristics of your new best friend here.

First of all, **"Zones"**.

Can you find the numbers on the map? They have been marked as 1, 2, 3, 4, 5, 6, 7, 8 and 9.

These numbers are used as a reference to the Zone system, which was initially set up by the London transportation department for travelling fare calculations but have now been adopted widely in the property industry. In general, when we say "premier location London" or "Central London", it means zone 1 most of the time. The higher the number for the zones, the farther out from central London it will be considered, which is a very important price index. You can generally expect a higher price for properties in London Zone 1 than properties in London Zone 4.

To put it simpler, think of this system as Beijing's Huan system; consider Zone 1 here as "Yi Huan" in Beijing, then you will get the idea.

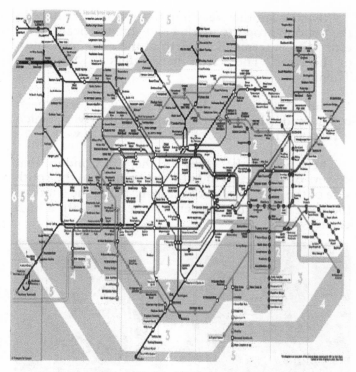

Secondly: Find the **RIVER!!** Can you see it?

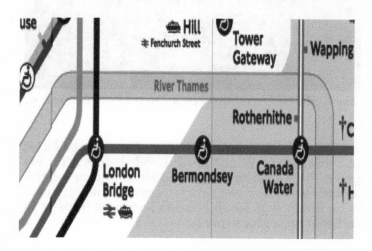

"River" is another very important reference here in the London property market and you will hear it a lot especially in terms like "north of the river" or "south of the river". The "river" here refers to "the River Thames".

Traditionally, "north of the river" has been considered to be better than "south of the river", which is reflected in the price of the properties as well.

There was a joke, years ago, here in London, that drivers of black cabs didn't want to cross to the south side of the river, one of the reasons being the south of the river has been considered to be poor with a high crime rate.

Black cabs used to refuse to go across the river in London.

Obviously, things and situations have changed a lot in recent years. Whilst north London does offer big green space such as Hampstead Heath, Primrose Hill and many of the royal parks in central London, there is no doubt that South London has more to offer in terms of huge green spaces.

South London generally offers properties with cheaper prices than North London. And also Wandsworth has the cheapest council tax rates in the whole of the country (this is the borough where Greenland bought the Ram Brewery). However, it doesn't mean that south of the river is "poorer" or full of dodgy areas, because it also has many expensive and lovely areas such as Wimbledon, Clapham and areas that are currently undergoing huge transformation such as Battersea.

The only thing that you'll notice once you have a look at the tube map again is that there are many more tube stations at the moment north of the River, than there are south of the River. Many people use this fact as a point to argue that "north of the river" is better than "south of the river" because of the more comprehensive transportation system.

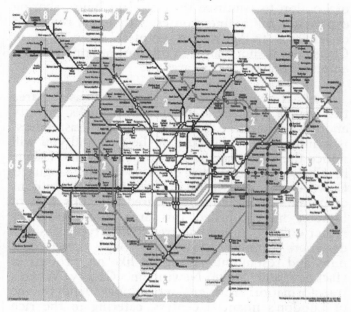

Can you see there are more tube stations "north of the river" and much fewer "south of the river"?

So next time when someone says, "This unit is north of the river," you know what he/she is talking about.

Thirdly: **"East" vs "West".**

Have you come across the concept of "East" and "West" yet (for the London property market)? If not, then you need to pay attention to what you are about to read next.

The "West" of the city is a harbour for old money, ancient families, the middle and upper classes (yes, you can still hear this word "class" in modern Britain). The streets of Notting Hill, Hammersmith, Fulham, Shepherds Bush, etc., are pounded by the wheels of sporty buggies and UGG-booted feet. Young graduates from Cambridge, Oxford, Nottingham and many other ancient cities of learning, flock to this area of London to continue their student house-sharing experience, but in finer houses, with higher rents and easier access to Waitrose. A recent TV show "Made in Chelsea" was shot mainly in this part of London, with emphasis on the Chelsea area.

"East" is newer. In the old days, this was the area that people typically associated with docks, poverty and high crime rate. The popular soap "Eastenders" is mainly shot in this part of the city, and you will notice the difference between this show and "Made in Chelsea" even if you don't speak the language. However, the new wealth of the City and the billions of pounds of investments poured into this part of London has propelled this area into modernity rather quickly. Young and trendy arty types; fashion designers running studios off Brick Lane; cool pubs and restaurants spring up like mushrooms in Hackney and Stoke Newington; Canary Wharf's transformation from an empty lonely land to one of London's financial centers, catering to the rich bankers with fat wallets; the world famous Olympics site, etc... all of which have transformed the "East". Coupled with the cheaper price tags and high demand of rental from the professional groups, this part of London has become the investors' favourite in the recent years. Companies like ABP, Alibaba, etc., all have a presence in this part of London.

A couple of days ago, a follower of my we-chat account left me a message on the system, "I have bought a property near Stratford area a couple of years ago, how is that area doing now?" (for your reference, Stratford is in East London.) Well, according to Zoopla's report, property prices in Stratford area have grown by 6.5% compared to one year ago (June 2015 compare to June 2014), 25.49% compared to two years ago; 29.31% compared to three years ago, 33.27% compared to four years ago and 34.52% compared to five years ago.

Now, if we enlarge the area, as Stratford is only one of the 14 postal areas that are adjoining to the Olympic park, how is this whole area doing? Since the winning of the Olympic Games in 2005, this part of east London has grabbed a great deal of attention from all sorts of investors and the area has been booming. Back in 2013, 8 years after the winning, the average price for this area had increased by £92,000 at a rate of 45%, with Dalston as the fastest growing spot. 2 years later, in 2015, the average property price in this area is £378,884, comparing to £206,191; we are looking at an increase rate of 84%!

Simply put, think of "West" and "East" in London as "Pu Xi" and "Pu Dong" in Shanghai, and you will have a rough idea.

Strangely, the only thing is that people in London do care about where you live more than you think. In Chinese culture, we like to greet people with, "Have you eaten today?" then, "How much money do you earn?"; whereas here in London, people greet you with, "So, where do you live?" True Londoners will tend to sum you up work wise, income wise, etc., purely from your answer. However, this is also changing, albeit, gradually.

Hence, it is very important for you to have some basic understanding of the "North/South, West/East" concept so that if you are buying a self-use unit, you know where to look depending on your preference: is it in the old part of the city with history or the new part of with vibrant energy? To live among a higher density of locals or among international culture; to choose to live nearer to the public transportation system areas or closer to large public spaces and parks?

On the other hand, if you are buying as an investment, then now you know that different parts of London will have more chances to offer you different types of tenants, ranging from the graduates, the arty types, the bankers to young families and immigrants, etc.

Fourthly: **Postcodes**

This is another very important reference that you cannot ignore — the postcodes.

This alphanumeric system was initially introduced by Royal Mail to aid the sorting out of the mail distribution and has been used widely in many other fields.

In the UK property industry nowadays, this system has been widely used to indicate the price difference and the location of the property.

Pay attention to all the developments or properties that you have been given; somewhere in the brochure or factsheet, you will always find the existence of this alphanumeric reference, such as "SE9", "SW1", "SW11 3DY". If you are an advanced level property investor and are following UK property market reports, you might have already come across quite a few articles or analysis purely based on the postcodes.

So what does it mean to you? And how does this relate to your property buying process?

Simply put, from the first part of the postcode, you will be able to tell the rough location of the property straightaway. If it starts with N, NW, E, SE, EC, WC, W, SW and SE, it means the property is in London, and it also indicates the rough location within London – N - north London; NW - north west London; E - east London; SE - south east London; EC - central east London; WC - central west London; W - west London, SW -south west London and SE - south east London.

London Postcode map

If the first part of the postcode you were given did not appear in the above list, then this property is based in another city.

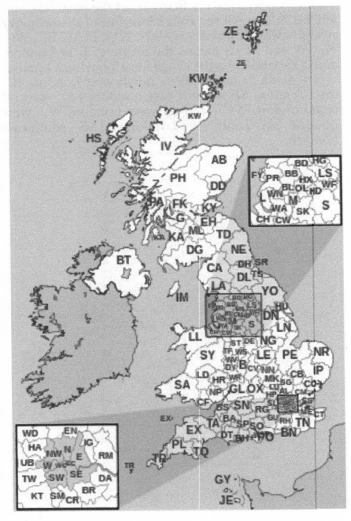

Use this map to get an idea of which city the property is based.

The combination of the door number and the full postcode will give you the exact address of the property. For instance: 10, SW1A 2AA is the exact and only address for 10 Downing Street.

The postcode system has also been used as an index for property prices with growing popularity. There are now numerous reports, news and articles on the rich list of the postcodes, the average price range for various postcodes, etc.

A basic understanding of this is a great start for you to understand the language of the UK property industry.

Other terms that you will possibly come across are "boroughs" and some of the specific "areas" such as Chelsea, Knightsbridge, Wimbledon, and Canary Wharf, etc. The latter is easier, as most of the time you can refer back to the London tube map and use the Zone rule (the further into the city, the higher the price) for reference.

These two terms are used most frequently in identifying the upcoming areas and hot areas:

"Borough" is like a small city with its own governments, schools, centers, suburbs and sense of identity. And London has 33 of these boroughs, or cities, within it.

Step Three: Back to the basics and find the RIGHT location for YOU!

Once you are confident that you are speaking the same language as the UK property professionals and insiders, you need to go back to the basics again in order to find the RIGHT location for YOU.

"Back to basics" here refers to the eight questions in chapter one.

It's all about YOU questionnaire

Question One:
Why do YOU want to buy a property in the UK?

Question Two:
How much is YOUR budget?

Question Three:
What's YOUR time line?

Question Four:
What's YOUR travelling arrangement?

Question Five:
How well do YOU know the UK?

Question Six:
What is YOUR biggest concern?

Question Seven:
Do YOU have a location in mind?

Question Eight:
How much can YOU afford to lose?

Let's say your answers are, "I want to buy a property in London because my daughter is about to start her three year undergraduate course at Imperial College in 9 months' time. I want her to move into the new flat around the start of the semester, I don't want her to commute too much, so this flat must be close to the university. I have a budget of 2 million pounds for a two-bedroom apartment and I can stretch my budget to 2.5 million if the property is right. I am a ready cash buyer with money already in my London bank account. I am OK to fly in if you give me a couple of days' notice if you need me to be there. I need to see the property before I put down the reservation fee. My biggest concern is the safety of my daughter; this place must be safe and have security doors and concierge services. I have been to London many times for business trips in the past 5 years."

With clear answers like this, it will be much easier for your chosen agent to narrow down the location search for you. You probably will be given some options in EC, WC, Zone 1, north of the river and within the boroughs of City, Westminster, Chelsea & Kensington and Tower Hamlets. The fact that you have been to London many times for business trips in the past 5 years will give you a great advantage in understanding your chosen agent's advice and language. You might still need your agent to go through the characteristics of the above chosen locations to narrow down the ones that you truly feel comfortable with.

Besides this, there are a couple of pitfalls that you should try to avoid when choosing a location, as specially pointed out by David Smith from Octagon Development Limited.

"Don't just put down the reservation fee if the estate agent or the developer told you that there are a few excellent schools nearby or there is a world-class golf club in the area." Because their existence does not mean that your children will be definitely admitted to the school or you are sure to get a membership card to that club. The world famous golf club can have a waiting list up to 30 years and a good schools can start their admission registration a couple of years in advance with no guarantee of acceptance.

"Don't think better value for money equals great investment return." Some of the properties are perfect for family use, but would not necessarily give you great return as an investment. You need to figure out exactly "what you do want". However, the general rule is to go for a nice house in a nicer area rather than a massive house on a side road or in a less desirable area.

3 Steps for Finding YOUR perfect Location! Location! Location!

Step One: Get the big picture.

Step Two: Make the London tube map your best friend and get familiar with terms like "zone", "postcode", "south or north of the river", "west or east", "boroughs" and some specific names for some areas.

Step Three: Back to the basics and find the right location for YOU!

OK, now you know why you are buying, what you are buying, where you are buying... What's the Next Big Thing?

Chapter Four
Do YOUR Research

"I say there is no darkness but ignorance"
-- William Shakespeare

If you are thinking about skipping this chapter, think again!

When I discussed this chapter with one of my clients, she questioned me. "What's the point of this chapter? They are buyers, who rely on you to do the research, now you are telling them to do research themselves? So what's the point of using your services then? Besides, most of them don't speak English, how will you expect them to carry out the research?"

Before you nod and agree with her comments, let me ask you some questions.

"How do you know who to use, whose advice to trust, or even whether that person is qualified to give you any advice?" The client who I mentioned above has known me for a few years and has bought a few properties from me. She can rely on my research because she knows I will do a good job. But if you don't know who you will use to help you with this property search, don't you need to at least do some research to find the professionals who you can trust and who will do a good job for you?

When presented with many options for properties in different areas, and you have no one to turn to for help and advice, won't you wish you knew a simple system of research that you could rely on to help you come to the best decision? Or even when you have someone you can trust, won't you wish you could at least know something about it so that you won't trust that person with complete blindness? At the end of the day, we are talking about your money here.

When you start the property buying process, most likely you will find it different from what is going on in your own country. Don't you wish you could find the best solicitor with the most reasonable price? Don't you wish you could know more about the procedure, to feel a sense of involvement and most importantly what exactly is going on?

After you have purchased the property, most of the time, the people that helped you before will stop there, and you will be on your own. Wouldn't it be nice if you knew what was going to happen next so that you will feel more secure?

The questions can go on and on, but the key message I want to stress here is this – no one likes to stay in the dark. Your own knowledge is the candle that you will be holding in your hand while research is that magic match to light this candle.

"If I had nine hours to chop down a tree,
I'd spend the first six sharpening my ax."
Abraham Lincoln

Like Abraham Lincoln said, preparation is the key and you do not want to rush this.

There are many things and aspects that you need to do research on before you take any solid action.

Before you are going to make the decisions about which property to buy, you need to research the right agent (this person is very important, I will talk about this separately in a while). Next you need to get your mortgage sorted out; if you are using a broker, then you need to do your research and decide on which one to use as you will be needing to share a lot of personal financial information with him/her; if you are using a bank, then you need to do your research and decide on which bank will offer you the best terms and which product to take from that particular lender. You can either purely rely on the chosen professional's advice or you can do some research on your own to explore deeper. I would always recommend my clients to do the latter and will advise you to do the same here, too.

In the meantime, you also need to do your research to decide on the solicitor that you are going to use. The UK property buying and selling process requires both the seller and buyer to have a solicitor representing them. Your chosen agent and the developer will normally recommend a solicitor firm to you. But YOU are going to make the decision of using it or not, and if I were you, I would at least do some research in advance on the general market rate, background on the recommended solicitor firm, etc. Wouldn't you do the same?!

Once the property sale starts, you will not know how long the process is going to take, how much extra money is going to be spent, and what kind of common problems you can expect if you do not do your research.

If the transaction is moving rather slowly and is behind schedule, you will not know how to push, who to push, or what to do to speed things up if you don't do the research.

Upon completion, how do you know the property is yours if you are still in your country and have not even visited the UK again since you chose the unit? How do you know how to let it out, how to sell it again, how to manage it? What is the market rate for all of those services and who can provide those reliable services?

Those are just a few of the questions that you will probably ask yourself with the progress of the buying process. The answers to them again are a combination of professional advice and your own research results.

You see, as much as I want to make things simpler and easier for you, the truth is the more research you do, the more you know, the better the decision you will make, and the more comfortable you'll be with the entire process.

However, the one thing that deserves your greatest attention is to find THE PEOPLE that can truly help you, and you need to get this RIGHT!

"I will always choose a lazy person to do a difficult job... because he will find an easy way to do it!"
- Bill Gates

I do not completely agree with Bill Gates on this, especially since the industry we are talking about here is very different. However, I do agree with him that to get a difficult job done, you need to find the right person! May he/she be lazy, may he/she be creative, and may he/she be disciplined... he/she must possess certain traits required for that particular role.

In your UK property investing process, there are some key people you need to find, namely: property agent, developer, solicitor, and mortgage provider/ broker. And I will teach you how to identify the right person with basic research.

Let's start with the "property agent", the person that will help you to find your dream property. To complete the difficult job of finding the right one for you, that person needs to be qualified, experienced, eager, a good listener, a good networker and most importantly, has to have integrity. If you find that person; you are 80% there.

Keep doing what you're doing in searching for this right person: exhibitions, books, blogs, reputable companies, friends' recommendations etc. Then you can narrow down the search based on the following two questions first: "Is the person qualified? Is the company regulated?"

In the UK, it is possible for anyone to set up, at any time, as an estate agent, and they do not need to be qualified or belong to either of the professional bodies to be able to start their practice. You need to ask yourself are you comfortable with this? Are you confident to entrust your money to someone like this?

Therefore do some research, find out whether this person has been qualified either by NAEA (National Association of Estate Agents), ARLA (The Association of Residential Letting Agents) or RICS (Royal Institution of Chartered Surveyors). If the person that you are seeking advice from has at least one of those qualifications, then you know that he/she has the professional knowledge you require and understands his/her responsibilities and codes of practice. If the company is regulated, then when things go wrong, you know you have a place to go for help or to complain.

With this as a good starting point, you can then move on to research this person's experience by either asking directly or looking at their professional profile, either on their company website or LinkedIn profile, etc., asking people that he/she worked with previously to see what kind of feedback you are getting... I am not asking you to be nosy and invade their personal privacy, instead I am only advising you to do just the right amount of research to know a bit more about that person who is potentially going to help you to spend a rather large amount of money in a foreign county. I do not want to rely on someone to find me a property if that person only stays in that country for a couple of months and has only been in the property industry for 3 months. Unless there is a very good reason behind it, such as he/she has been investing himself/herself successfully in the past, I would not feel comfortable letting that person give me advice on what to buy and what not to buy! Neither should you!

Ask the right questions before starting a professional relationship with a person, do your research in advance to see whether you like what you see or hear. 3-year-old children are known for asking lots of questions (Why? Why? Why?) and you should follow their lead when picking an agent.

Do your research, and then you will also understand how the UK property industry works. There are three main groups of property professionals who are active on the market currently. One of the groups is called "local agents", who have deep rooted knowledge, databases and relationships with the local market they are representing; the second group of professionals are the ones who are more geared towards the new developments and overseas exhibitions, they tend to focus on the general picture, bigger trends and what's coming next; the last group of professionals are the ones who are called "buying agents", who charge their buyers a fee (normally it is a little payment first then a percentage of the total house price upon completion) in exchange for their services in searching for the right property for the clients on the market in general.

If you are an experienced buyer with great knowledge of the UK and a clear idea of which location you want to buy, then you probably will benefit from the local agent more. As you build up a good relationship with them, you will find it even easier to resell your property or rent it out in the future.

If you are not that experienced but with some knowledge, then the second group of professionals will possibly be your best bet as they will lead you in the right direction. All you need to do is to make sure you have done all the right research on this person/ company and are confident that they can build up your trust.

If you want to have less hassle and want to get access to everything that's on the market and to have someone hold your hand the entire time, then you probably need to consider using the third group of professionals. But again, do your research first!

Now you have decided on which agent to use, that person has recommended you a few developments, how do you know which developer to trust? Mr David Smith from Octagon Development Limited provided the following four points for you to base your research on: One, find out how long this developer has been established! You should be a bit more cautious if the developer hasn't been in operation for longer than 5 years as some of the developers might just do a couple of sites and disappear. Two, will the property come with some types of warranty? If so, what are they? What's the length? And what do they cover? Three, what's the developer's background? What sort of projects they have done in the past? You should be able to research this information either on their website or from their company brochure. Four, if you are consciously, worried or unsure, the last resort you can use is to go through the company's accounts, although access to these can be difficult at times.

Next is the solicitor. How do you know you have found the right solicitor? What kind of research you should be doing? Believe it or not, the first thing you need to do is to fight "Fraud". Ms Mei Lu, Co-founder of LuOliphant Solicitors LLP stresses the importance of this matter, especially to our International buyers. "Every REAL law firm will have a registration number, which can be checked out at www.sra.org.uk", Ms Lei shares this simple but deadly useful tip. Ms Polly from Gawor & Co then provides us with another simple solution to decide on which one to use afterwards – ask the solicitor some right questions! This way, you can get a sense of whether they have the experience in that specific field. Although the solicitors all need to go through similar training, their work experience does make a difference in their practice, such as some solicitors are more experienced with new build development, some are with second hand market, while others are with international buyers. An example of a good question to ask will be, "If I want to pass on my property to the next generation, can I do it? Can I do it without any tax complications?" The answer you are expecting should not be just a straightforward "yes" or "no", you should expect a good solicitor to be able to go a bit further and provide a more comprehensive answer. Another question you can also ask is, "What are the main concerns and questions that clients often raise?" Answers to this will give you an insight into their level of knowledge, experience and competency. What's even better is that while you are doing this, you will get a clearer overview of the process yourself. Kill two birds with one stone.

If you decided on using a mortgage broker, as you will need to provide a lot of very personal information to that person, thus the right research from your end will be crucial too. Mr Stephen Brown from Overseas Mortgage Broker Ltd. suggested two key areas that you must research on: one, their qualifications and which professional association body do they belong to and two, their data protection procedures and rules.

The general rule is that the more you are going to rely on the professional's help, the more you need to do research on that professional. The less you are going to rely on the professional's help, the more you need to do research on everything else.

> *"I couldn't repair your brake, so I made*
> *your horn louder"*
> **Steven Wright**

If you cannot turn yourself into a property professional at the time you are buying the property, do your research and make up for it.

Here, I am going to share some great places for you to look.

We are very lucky in the way that technology has made it possible for us to access almost everything about anything at any time, anywhere. For you, you can use online and offline methods to look for the information you will need.

Online:

For UK news, you can go to:

www.bbc.co.uk/news;
www.thetimes.co.uk;
www.independent.co.uk;
http://www.theguardian.com/uk-news

The above four websites have been considered to provide trustworthy and quality news on the UK, although the readership of the Times, the Independent and the Guardian are not as high as some of the other UK news websites according to the latest Ofcom (UK news regulations authority) 2014 report on news consumption in the UK.

For UK property professional bodies, go to:

http://www.nfopp.co.uk;
www.nhbc.co.uk;
http://www.tpos.co.uk/index.php.

Don't be scared when you open these pages because they look too professional. All you need to know is that on the first website you will be able to find the professional bodies that are issuing qualifications for sales and letting professions. On the second website, you need to know this is insurance related especially to the off-plan new developments; normally it comes in a 10 years warranty. On the last one, all you need to know is that this is a place you can go and complain and ask for your rights if things go wrong and the agents you are using are regulated.

For knowing the UK like a local, you can go to websites like:

www.timeout.com
(things to do and places to go)
www.booking.com
(hotels with good bargain price)
www.lastminute.com
(booking cheap hotels, flights, etc)

For searching properties in the UK, you can go to websites like:

www.zoopla.com
www.rightmove.com

Two property search engines that pretty much cover all the properties in UK; recently, there is also a new property portal that has gone live, which you can also check out: www.onthemarket.com.

For more community type of websites, go to:

www.powerapple.com (Chinese)
www.honglingjin.co.uk (Chinese)
www.hereinuk.com (Chinese)

For the latter two, you can follow their we-chat as well.

For local property markets, especially in London, there are some major magazines you can search out:

London Property Review
South
The Wharf newspaper
Abode2

You can also visit their websites.

Three major newspapers have a home and properties section:

The Sunday Times
Thursday's Evening Standard
Metro newspaper

Last but not least: your legs – what we also call the "No 11 bus".

If it is possible, when you are in the UK or if your kids are in the UK, ditch the cars, use public transportation and walk around the areas that you are going to buy for a good day or half a day.

Walk through the various main streets, sideways, public parks, local shops, restaurants etc; chat with the people in the local cafes, pubs, and local estate agents; wait outside the tube station/train station to observe the types of people that are commuting in that area; look for signs of the development of the areas such as the brands of the parked cars on the residential streets, the types of supermarkets in the area, any new developments building in the area, etc.

What you see during this walk will say a lot of things about that particular area that you won't be able to see otherwise.

Like everything else in life, every suggestion has its own challenges. The difficulties you will be facing even if you are given the right resources are: how to overcome the language barrier? How to not feel overwhelmed with all this information? How do you take the negative comments on the community website? And how are you going to hear your own voice?

The language barrier is probably the top challenge on your list. At the end of the day, if you do not understand the language, you cannot move forward that much. The good news is that with the growing number of Chinese buyers in the UK, a small number of people have started to work on filling this gap. You can obtain a UK property market report from the major agents now, and some of the developers have also had a Chinese language translation tool installed, such as http://www.octagon.co.uk, who have been developing beautiful luxurious houses since 1980.

I, personally also write regular blogs on my own website www.sjwukproperties.com. And have a we-chat account, "Let's buy a property in the UK", (you can search "sjwuk2015" on your wechat) to provide analyzed UK property news in simple language on a daily basis.

The gap is still there, but the gap is getting smaller and smaller.

What if you feel overwhelmed with all the information from all the resources that I have suggested above, and maybe from the resources that your family and friends recommended? The worst thing is if you spend all your time struggling with covering all of the widespread information without too much time thinking about it. If this is the case, don't panic and try not to worry about it too much. After all, you are not a professional; well, not just yet. Take it easy and slow, build up your own references based on things that matter to you and your decision the most, and your mind will be trained to attract the right information for you. For instance, if your reason for buying a property is for an investment with the primary goal of wanting to get a stable monthly income, with no intention to sell it in the foreseeable future, then your reference will be the upcoming areas, areas that the government is spending money on, areas that are creating more jobs, with a degree of mobile population, areas that have easy transportation accessibility. Your other references will be any changes to the landlords' taxes, responsibilities etc. Once you set up these references, your subconscious mind will start working on it and you will become gradually attracted to those types of information. Have you ever had the experience of not seeing any husky puppies, then one day your best friend gets a husky puppy, and you start to see husky puppies wherever you go? Similar things will happen to you in your property buying experience once you have set up your own references.

If your reason for buying a property is for your daughter to study next year in London, it is not difficult to figure out that your references will be transportation links, the London crime rate, where the safe areas are, what streets you probably want to avoid especially when it's getting dark, policies on inheritance tax, changes of rules on how to transfer the name of the title from you to your daughter (if you didn't buy it initially under her name but want her to have it later on). Then every time you are using the above resources, your subconscious mind will lead you to pay attention to that type of news.

Again, go back to the basics – the eight questions that I wanted you to ask yourself in chapter one – and you will build up your own references sooner and easier than you would otherwise.

Prepare yourself! Although you perceive the UK as a fine place to live and invest in, the reality is that a lot of people still complain about a lot of things a lot of the time. I am always amazed by how many negative comments I come across on the community websites or expats' websites. You need to learn how to take this with a pinch of salt. On one hand, those complaints might potentially reflect what you are feeling, because to live in, or invest in another country is not as easy as buying a bottle of milk in the supermarket. It involves a lot of financial commitment and emotional ups and downs. Reality rarely lives up to one's imagination. But on the other hand, always remember things are different for different people. Listen to it but use your own judgment with the research you have done.

I mentioned earlier on that once you have found the right professional agent to help you with your research, you are 80% there. Yes, that's correct! To find the right person means a great deal in the property buying process in the UK. However, you still need to RESPECT and TRUST your own voice. You and the agent you have chosen are different people. There is no other person who knows what is best for you and your money better than you.

Take the facts and figures that he/she gives you, respect his/her opinion, but as you and I both know, his /her opinion is still his/her opinion, not yours. Use what he/she gives you, coupled with the research you have done, find your own voice and follow it; that's the key to the best decision for you in this UK property buying process.

Although "research" can seem to be a hopeless process for you, guess what? Once you follow the simple rules of readjusting your attitude, setting up your own references and using the reliable search resources, it will become less scary and I trust you can do this!

Chapter Five
Money, Money, Money

At last, it is the chapter you have been waiting for!

I don't blame you if you chose to start the book with this chapter. Whether buying a property in the UK is still a dream you have or you are ready to make the move, it is absolutely sensible to know the costs that will be involved, and when you need to pay them.

I always wanted to have a puppy when I was little, but my parents never got me one. "Too much responsibility and too expensive," they always said to me. "We don't have the money for it and you are not ready for the responsibility." At that age, I always thought those were just really weak excuses that made absolutely no sense. What do they mean by saying it's too expensive? You could buy a puppy for around 20 pounds (around 300 RMB; those are the times when pounds were so strong against RMB) back then and I just needed to share some of my food, which I was so willing to do. Puppies don't even need clothes or shoes. Why did they keep telling me it was too expensive to have a puppy?

It was three years ago, when I had my first dog in London – a lovely miniature schnauzer – when I started to understand my parents' advice and reluctantly agreed with them that to have a puppy involves a lot of responsibility and it is not as inexpensive as I thought.

Spending £700 to get the puppy home with me was just a start! There are monthly fixed expenses after that, such as food, insurance, dog walking, etc. (to keep him fit and happy while both of us are at work during the day); there are some other fixed expenses which are not monthly but also require a regular frequency such as worming tablets, injections, flea treatments, grooming etc.; Snowy (our dog) doesn't have a passport yet (which will also cost a fair amount of money), which means when we go on holiday overseas, he is going on a luxurious holiday too, here in the UK on a beautiful farm together with a group of other dogs. Great exercises that come with a high price tag. Last summer, he had a grass seed stuck in one of his paws, which led to inflammation and then led to hundreds of pounds of bills for the treatment. Touch wood, we are very lucky as we bought insurance and we have always kept a close eye on him. One of our neighbours' dogs on the contrary was less fortunate; he got knocked over by a car while he ran off to chase a squirrel across the street, and it led to thousands of pounds of medical bills to get him right again. Those are the unexpected costs of having a puppy.

"What are you talking about? We are not discussing puppies here, we are talking about buying a property in the UK, just cut to the chase and get on with it!" you might be screaming loudly in your head by now.

Believe it or not, I have actually already started talking about it. Buying a puppy is very similar to buying a property in the UK. It involves a lot of responsibility and a lot of costs not just at the beginning, but also afterwards; some of them are expected, others are not. You need to be able to calculate the costs that you can expect and prepare for the costs that are unexpected.

Buying a property in the UK has a "puppy effect".

Let's start with **getting the "puppy" home**. In the UK, the cost and payment terms are different between buying a new build property and a second hand unit. For a new build off-plan unit, there are a few upfront costs that you need to clear before the seller can release you the keys. There are two major costs you need to pay special attention to: the deposit and stamp duty. The rest range from under a hundred pounds to no more than a few thousand pounds.

Once you see the property (I stress here again: we are talking about an off-plan new development) you like, the first payment you need to make is the "reservation fee" which you pay to the developer. Reservation fees vary from a few hundred pounds to a few thousand pounds, depending on the value of the property. This is the proof that you are serious about this and as a result, most of the time, the **reservation fee** is non-refundable if you change your mind afterwards. If the reservation fee is non-refundable, do ask an agreement from the developer to remove the property from the market for certain amount of time – 6 weeks for instance and not showing it to anyone else. This is to avoid the situation that the developer will sell it on after taking the reservation fee.

It sounds like an evil thing, and it does not happen that often. But when it happens, it can be frustrating. You want to try as hard as you can to prevent this happening to you. Don't you agree?

Once you have reserved the unit, then you need to crack on and get it moving as soon as you can, as the developer will normally give you a deadline for the exchange of contract. (Usually it is around one month's time.)

The next immediate costs are related to the solicitor and mortgage. Once you have chosen the solicitor and put down the reservation fee, you need to inform your solicitor you want them to go ahead and represent you. In order to do this, the solicitor will normally ask you to transfer a small amount of money (usually a few hundred pounds) to them before they start the paperwork. The rest of the fee normally will only need to be cleared upon completion. The total cost for each case is mostly based on the price of the property and the intricacy of the deal (the price range you will be looking at is between a few hundred pounds and a few thousand pounds). You should get the price quotation from your solicitor at a very early stage.

If you need to arrange a mortgage, then you should know that the lenders will usually charge an arrangement fee. The exact amount varies depending on the product. A higher lending fee may also be payable if you borrow a large percentage of the value of the property. (The fee related to the mortgage arrangement varies from a few hundred pounds to a few thousand pounds.) You do not need to pay for this until the mortgage is in place upon completion. Check with your lender or your mortgage broker. Before granting you a mortgage, your lender will also require you to pay for a valuation of the property, since they have to be sure that the house in question will form sufficient security against their loan. This payment is generally required when you submit your initial application. (The figure you are looking at here is a few hundred pounds to a couple of thousand pounds.)

Surveyors are a service that you can choose to do or not to do if you are buying a new build property, unlike second hand units. A lot of people choose not to use a surveyor and a small group of buyers just carry out a new-build snagging survey, which is to pick up mistakes such as plumbing the hot to the cold tap or poorly finished painted work; your independent inspector will also be able to arrange for the developer to sort out any defects found. You see, the majority of buyers choose not to use this service because they can either have a check themselves or their agent will do this for them with a small charge.

The next immediate cost will be the "deposit". This is the part that requires the majority of the money before the completion, and it varies from developer to developer. In general, you will be required to put down 10% - 20% of the purchase price upon exchange of the contract. For a lot of developments, you will also be required to pay a further 10% of the total property price 6 months (depending on the developer) after the exchange of the contract; and some will require you to put down a further 10% of the purchase price after another 6 months (once again, depending on the developer). And the remaining amount (the 70% - 90% that you haven't paid) will need to be in place before completion.

The payment term usually is clearly stated in the reservation form and told to you in advance by the developer and your agent. If you do not have clear and full information on this or you have anything you are not sure about, ask for it and make sure everything is in writing.

There is another major cost you need to bear in mind – the SDLT (short for Stamp Duty Land Tax), and this needs to be paid before the completion with your own cash rather than via mortgage arrangements.

The stamp duty rate has recently been changed in December 2014 from a single rate for the entire price of a property to increasing rates for each portion of the price.

Consideration	Rate (Paid Portion in band)
Up to £125,000	0%
From £125,001 to £250,000	2%
From £250,001 to £925,000	5%
From £925,001 to £1,500,000	10%
Over £1,500,00	12%

Current residential property stamp duty rate (www.gov.uk)

You do not need to pay anything if the property you are buying is under £125,000; you need to pay 2% on the next £125,000, 5% on the next £675,000, 10% on the next £575,000 and 12% on the rest (above £1.5 million).

Let's work out an example to make things simpler: If you buy a property for £275,000, you will be looking at £3,750 for stamp duty payment.

Which is made up of:

£0	For the first £125,000
+ £2,500	On the next £125,000 - (£125,000 x 2% = £2,500)
+ £1,250	On the remaining £25,000 – the property price is £275,000 minus the first £125,000, minus another £125,000 = £25,000; 5% x £25,000 = £1,250
	£0 + £2,500 + £1,250 = £3,750 – The Stamp Duty

Top tip: if you hate math, you can use this link to work out how much you will pay for the stamp duty. **http://www.hmrc.gov.uk/tools/sdlt/land-and-property.htm**

Your solicitor will be acting for you to get this money paid on your behalf at a small fee, which will also be listed in the price quotation they offered you at the very beginning.

There will be some other small costs that usually occur such as a local search fee, land registration fee, money transfer fee, etc. In normal conditions, those costs are around £100 or less, each.

Don't get too worried about not being able to remember all these costs, your chosen solicitor will provide you with a breakdown of almost all the cost except the ones they cannot oversee or control, such as the lending arrangement fee for the bank or the surveyor fee if you choose so.

If the property you are about to buy is a second hand unit, then the payments will be quite different.

First of all, if you like a property that you see and you want to reserve it, with a second hand unit, the developer has disappeared from the scene a long time ago. Thus, you will not be reserving the unit from the developer; instead, you will be reserving with the agent that is working on behalf of the seller. The agent will decide on the amount of reservation fee that you need to pay, which normally is a few hundred pounds (depending on the company policy and the value of the property). However, in a lot of cases, you do not even need to put down a reservation fee because the agent has some professional relationship with either the seller or you, or they simply decided not to take any reservation fees from anyone.

The solicitor fee, mortgage arrangement fee, valuation fee and surveyor fee will be similar to the off plan properties.

However, you will want to seriously consider taking up the surveyor services for the second hand property, as this is vital to help you understand if there are any issues with the property before you buy. Paying for a good survey could save you from making a huge mistake of buying if the property has a major problem that you cannot afford to fix. Also, it gives you a powerful reason to re-negotiate down the price or ask the seller to fix the issues before you move in.

There are three main types of surveys you will be looking at: the condition report, which covers the most basic survey you can get at a price range of a few hundred pounds (normally under £500); homebuyer's report (the most popular one), that gives you a more detailed report with highlights of problems with the property such as dampness or subsidence, at a price range of a few hundred pounds (normally around £500) or the most thorough, a buildings survey (also called structure survey) at a price range of around £1,000 or above.

You should also expect the deposit and final payment to be very different from off-plan properties. You will usually need to put down a deposit (normally it's 10% of the purchase price, which will be confirmed by your solicitor) upon exchange of contract and then all the rest upon completion.

I think it's worthwhile to point out another big difference here for you as well - time scale. With the off plan property, although sometimes you need to pay 30% of the purchase price, that has been broken down typically to 12-18 months' time scale, and it also gives you some time to arrange the rest of the financing, especially if the site is to be completed in 2 to 3 years' time. Whereas with the second hand property, if everything goes smoothly, you are looking at around 3 months' time to reach the stage of exchanging the contract and a few weeks longer for the completion (sometimes even on the same day or just a few days apart), which means you really need to get the cash and the mortgage ready in a relatively short period of time.

Stamp duty is based on the purchase price of the property, thus there will be no difference whether you are buying a second hand unit or an off plan new development.

How much will you lose if the deal falls through before the exchange of contract?

A couple of years ago, one of my clients decided to go for a two-bedroom Victorian conversion apartment in London. We did everything right, we calculated all the potential costs, had the mortgage agreement in principle ready, the solicitors were working towards an agreed exchange date and the surveyor had also provided the homebuyer's report. Then the exchange date never came. Instead, it was just pushed back further and further without any clear explanation. Situations like this can be daunting; my client at that time told me that she was devastated and felt like she was going to be dumped by her husband for no obvious reasons and she deserved to know!

Yes, we do deserve to know, however, the reality is that the seller rarely will tell you the real reason they are pulling out. Instead of dwelling on figuring out the reason, count your losses and move on fast to prevent more damage, stay realistic, practical and positive.

Because in the UK, before the exchange of contract, no one is bound to this transaction legally, the seller or you (the buyer) can pull out anytime without giving any reasons with no further penalty.

So if this situation has unfortunately become inevitable, what will you be losing?

You will lose all the money that you have already spent, such as the solicitor fee for the work that has taken place (any reasonable firm will charge a percentage of the overall legal costs, which is based on the amount of work that has been carried out on the transaction), the surveyor fee and sometimes the mortgage arrangement fee. That's why I said earlier on, count your losses and move on fast to prevent the damage. If you can find another property straight away, you might be able to negotiate with the solicitor on their cost and carry the credit on to this new property transaction.

Now you have the "puppy", you brought it home. What will you do next?

You probably will go out and buy a bottle of dog shampoo, a bed, a comb, a dog towel, some food, some treats, some toys and things to set him up and make him comfortable. Then you probably will start to make appointments with all the people that are essential to keep him healthy and happy. You will probably register yourself with a local vet, get him a good insurance policy, and a dog walker if you need to work away from home most of the day.

It is very similar to what will happen to you and your money after you have the keys to your property in the UK.

First of all, you'll probably need to spend some money to set it up, whether it is for yourself to live in or to rent it out. You might need to renovate the place if you bought a second hand unit in not so good condition; you might need to buy a set of furniture for yourself or for your potential tenants (furnished property generally rents out quicker and at a higher price range).

Then you need to spend some money to keep it going. In the UK, landlords and tenants have very clear-cut responsibilities (well, in most of the cases). Landlords need to pay for bills that are related to property ownership such as service charge and ground rent; whereas the tenants need to pay for their own usage of all the bills related to the property, such as council tax, utility bills, TV licence, internet, telephone bill etc., unless pre-negotiated otherwise.

If you are living in the property as a sole tenant, then of course, you need to pay for all of the above.

What exactly are those costs? And how much, roughly, are they? I will make this as simple as possible as I have no intention to bore you with these house bills.

For some reason, quite a few of my clients were very confused about the council tax and the stamp duty, although the difference in numbers is pretty huge. **Stamp duty is the fee that you pay when you purchase the property** while **council tax is the fee that you pay to the local government** for the bin collections, street sweeping, etc. **after you buy it.** The rate is calculated into 8 different bands (From A to H) based on the assumed property value and the particular borough your property is in. In general, it ranges from under £1,000 per year to over £2,000 per year (England).

Band	Main part of the Borough	Wimbledon and Putney Commons Conservators' area*
A	£454.51	£472.76
B	£530.27	£551.57
C	£606.02	£630.36
D	£681.77	£709.15
E	£833.27	£866.73
F	£984.78	£1024.33
G	£1136.28	£1181.91
H	£1363.54	£1418.30

(Sample: Wandsworth council tax band charge)
Source: http://www.wandsworth.gov.uk/info/200262/council_tax_charge/5/how_much_is_council_tax/2)

Top tip: to find out which council tax band your property is, check out this website http://cti.voa.gov.uk/cti/inits. asp. Just type in your property's postcode, you will find out which band you need to pay for.

Utility bills generally involve water, electricity and gas bills, which purely depend on how much you have been using them; normally you will be looking at from under £100 to a couple of hundred pounds a month for a normal sized family home.

One of the potentially most expensive costs to run a property is the service charge (which only applies to new apartment and leasehold properties). It has become very common to calculate this in the format of price per square foot. For instance, if you bought a brand new apartment of 1000 square feet and were told that the service charge is £3 per square foot per year, then you are looking at a cost of £3,000 per year for the service charge. Generally speaking, the higher end your properties are, the more expensive your service charge will be. For the world renowned One Hyde Park development, you are looking at above £20 per square foot per year, which means you need to pay over £20,000 per year for a 1,000 square foot apartment!

Converted flats enjoy a great cost advantage in this area with a possible significant difference in the cost of not having a concierge or a swimming pool.

Ground rent also applies to leasehold properties and there is not much difference among new build, second hand apartments or converted flats, cost wise. You are generally looking at a few hundred pounds per year.

There are a few other costs you might incur such as a TV licence (currently £145.50 for a colour TV and £49 for a black and white TV. Source: *http://www. tvlicensing.co.uk/check-if-you-need-one/topics/tv-licence- types-and-costs-top2*), telephone and internet costs, etc. But as I said earlier on, for these types of costs that are related to personal usage, there is a general rule of whoever uses it needs to pay for it.

As much as we all want only good things to happen to us, we cannot have everything we want or have everything happen exactly the way we want. That's why we always need to be well prepared for unwanted things or situations.

Whether you are a homeowner or a landlord, you want to consider buying various types of insurance, just in case. Contents insurance, building insurance and rental guarantee are the three most commonly used insurance policies; none of them are overly expensive.

"A Dog is for life, not just for Christmas!" My parents were right when they said having a puppy was a huge responsibility that I was not ready for at that age. It is not fair for the dog if you decide to just dump him somewhere in the street when things don't work out for you. It is a lifetime commitment, especially for your dog.

On the contrary, having a property in a foreign country is less of a commitment. After the deal is completed, you can choose to live there, to rent it out or even to sell it on. There is no lifetime commitment and you have the freedom to choose whatever works for you... However, you do need to have an idea of the cost for each option.

If you want to rent out your property via an agent, then there will be a letting fee at a rate of around 10% (London) of the yearly rental income to be paid to your letting agent (usually it's a one off payment upon receiving the first month's rent), plus a monthly management fee at around 2.5% - 6% of the monthly rental income. Find out the rate your letting agent is charging and see whether you can get a better deal.

If you want to resell the property, you will be looking at three obvious costs: the selling agent's fee (usually between 1% and 2.5%), the solicitor fee (between a fewhundred and a few thousand) and the capital gains tax (for any property that is sold after 6th of April, 2015 and which was owned by an international buyer).

What if there are unexpected situations that happen, or a money-related issue that I have not touched on here? What would you do? And to whom should you turn for help?

Have you ever had any relationship problems before? And when that happened, what did you normally do? Did you keep it to yourself? Or did you ask your friends or his/her friends to figure out what was going on? And what should you do next?

Did you notice that people give you different advice? Your single friends tend to give you advice that normally will keep you single; your married friends tend to give you advice that normally will lead to a marriage; your friends who have been enjoying a good fulfilling relationship have a better chance to offer you tips on how to have the same thing; and friends in unhealthy relationships might give you advice on how not to have a relationship at all...

My point here is that you have to be very careful WHOM you ask advice from! In the UK property buying process, you need to be extremely careful and picky with who can give you advice on money and who cannot!

Remember: not everyone is qualified to give you advice on money! Ask to see their professional qualification before they offer to give you advice on money.

OK, no more costs; I have so far given you almost every cost that you can expect during this buying process. If you want, you can print out this table and tick it off along the way.

UK property buying cost check list

Tick Box	Name of the cost	What's the cost	Who is paying	When to pay
		BEFORE COMPLETION		
	Reservation fee	From a few hundred pounds to a few thousand pounds	You the buyer	Once you decide to buy
	Solicitor fee	From a few hundred pounds to a few thousand pounds	You the buyer	A small amount at the beginning, remaining upon completion
	Mortgage arrangement	From a few hundred pounds to a couple of thousand pounds	You the buyer	Upon completion
	Surveyor	From a couple of hundred pounds to a couple of thousand pounds	You the buyer	Before exchange of contract
	Deposit	10% - 30% of the purchase price (varies from development to development, different between new build and second hand)	You the buyer	Partially before exchange of contract and partially before completion
	Stamp Duty	Percentage of the purchase price	You the buyer	Upon completion
	Other costs	Local search fee, land registration fee, money transfer fee etc.	You the buyer	Upon completion
		AFTER COMPLETION		
	Service charge	From a few hundred pounds to a few thousand pounds	You the owner	Yearly (can set up payment plan)
	Ground rent	A few hundred pounds	You the owner	Yearly (can set up payment plan)
	Council tax	From a few hundred pounds to a couple of thousand pounds	Whoever is living in the property	Yearly (can set up payment plan)
	Gas, water and electricity	From under a hundred pounds to a couple of hundred pounds normally	Whoever is living in the property	Monthly (can set up payment plan)
	TV licence	£49 for black and white TV & £145.50 for colour TV	Whoever is watching TV	Yearly (can set up payment plan)
	Telephone, internet, Satellite TV	Normally is under £100 (depends on the service package you choose)	Whoever is using it	Monthly
	Contents insurance	A few hundred pounds to a few thousand pounds	You the owner	Yearly (can set up payment plan)
	Building insurance	A few hundred pounds to a few thousand pounds	You the owner	Yearly (can set up payment plan)
	Rental guarantee	A few hundred pounds to a couple of thousand pounds	You the owner	Yearly or the tenancy agreement length
	Letting fee	Around 10% of the yearly rental income	You the owner	Upon receiving the first month's rent
	Management fee	Around 2.5% - 6% of the monthly rental income	You the owner	Monthly
	Sales fee	Around 1% - 2.5% of the sales price	You the owner	Upon completion of the resale

Part Two

You Are Doing This!

Chapter Six

Buyers are from Mars and Everyone Else is From Venus

Now, you are really doing this! You have got all the answers to your questions, you've done the research and found the property that you would love to buy and you've put down the reservation fee.

And then suddenly you realise that you are not in this alone anymore, and you have got various people involved and you find this is getting more and more complicated.

The truth is: actually, the hardest part is over.

The search for the right property can take up a lot of time even for a local buyer. Before the invention of Zoopla and Rightmove, local people still needed to walk around their desired areas (after a long process of narrowing down to their final choices), register themselves with every single local agent and go through every single property they have, before they finally make the decision. Technology has made our lives much easier, but has also created some new challenges. In desirable areas, when the supply is lower than the demand, the stocks tend to move rather quickly; this is a huge disadvantage to our international buyers, especially for the ones that have to visit the property to be able to say that "YES" and make the commitment. I have seen far too many buyers go through such a long and emotional rollercoaster in the process of searching for the right one, and have always advised them to be prepared to make a quick decision if they think they feel right, even if they only started their search recently. Sometimes, even when the technology, people and money are on your side, time is not.

So, big congratulations to you if you have completed this stage and have now moved on to the next level to make this happen! And once you have reached this side of the tunnel, your biggest job is done. A small group of professionals will take over with the goal of completing the deal for you.

However, this doesn't mean you can just go out and play, leave everything behind and just wait for it to happen. You need to understand the difference between you and everyone else that is involved in this transaction to be able to monitor it; failing to do so might lead to a disastrous result.

Buyers are From Mars and Everyone Else is From Venus

There is a small group of professionals who will be directly involved in your property transaction: property agents, developers (if you are buying a new build), vendors (if you are buying a second hand property), solicitors (yours and the seller's), surveyors (from the bank or your own hired ones), lenders and mortgage brokers (if you are using one). Whether you like it or not, the differences between you and them are pretty big.

The first gap you will be facing is the language and cultural difference. As an international property buyer, you have a high chance of speaking a different language from the group of professionals you will be working with (unless you are lucky enough to find all the professionals that speak your mother tongue, too). The majority of my mainland Chinese clients find this very challenging and many of them have expressed their frustration to me on several occasions, directly and indirectly.

One time, when I was at a Hong Kong exhibition, I met this woman who wanted to buy a couple of houses off the site we were selling on the day; she could not speak any English or Cantonese, so, she had to stick with me that day, as I was the only one who could communicate with her. She wanted to buy, but she wasn't so sure about the legal process of buying, so I asked the solicitor (who is a very experienced English solicitor) to come and sit at the same table in order to answer some of her questions while I did the translation. It all went pretty well until at one point, there were other things that needed my attention for about 10 minutes; not that long for me, but obviously it was very long for an anxious buyer and a helpful solicitor who could not speak her language and had no clue what she was talking about. Upon my return, I could see the frustration on both of their faces and also the laughter and relief they had when they saw me! I have never felt that important! It turned out she was still talking to him loudly and slowly in Chinese while I was away, hoping that he could understand her.

There was another time, around summer last year; I was helping this young Chinese couple to find their dream home in the UK because three of their kids were going to school here. The wife spoke a little English, while the husband spoke none. I had huge respect for this couple, in their 40s, because they were already self-made multi-millionaires with an open mind and the courage to take on new challenges and seek a new way of life. And it is people like them who make me love what I do! To be part of their new exciting journey! On one of the house hunting days, the husband said to me, "Sally, I feel frustrated and out of control. In China, I know exactly what is going on, I can analyse things and make the best decision with the information I have at hand, and I can then communicate my ideas with people. Here I feel like I am deaf as I don't understand what they are talking about, even worse, I feel like I am mute as I can only express myself with my hand gestures and body language." For such a powerful man to say this and feel like this was such a shocking experience I swore to myself I would try my best to help them and people like them to make the UK property buying experience much easier.

Cultural difference is another factor that widens this first gap, which you as an international buyer will be facing. One of my favorite books is called Watching the English: The Hidden Rules of English Behaviour by Kate Fox, which was amusing, chatty and provided me with such a great reference in looking at the UK from a different and closer perspective. It made me understand that "there is different culture here in this nation and there are hidden rules that people's behaviours are based on" and many of those rules are different from ours. Such as: try not to contact the professionals after their working hours on their personal phone, although most of them will not give you their private number anyway, even though in China, sometimes we believe "where there is a will, there is a way"; Friday means Friday, the beginning of a weekend etc.... As a Chinese person myself, I mostly still worked as a Chinese person with my we-chat on 24/7 without thinking about it too much. Until one day, one of my young clients, a lovely graduate who had spent the past few years here in UK studying we-chatted me this: "Sally, just wanted to let you know that I have sent you the documents you required to your email box. Check it next week, as I understand it is the weekend now." That girl was so sweet that I still keep that message on my phone, but I still checked the documents that night anyway.

The point here is not asking you not to contact the professionals on Fridays or not calling their cellphone if they gave you one. The point is to understand and respect the difference, and push it at the right time; by showing your respect and understanding, you will make people want to work for you even more.

The second gap you as an international buyer will be facing is the different needs and intentions behind each individual professional role.

You, the buyer, are paying and you possibly want:

A. To negotiate down the prices as low as you can – less cost;
B. The deal to go as smoothly as possible – less hassle;
C. The seller to provide you with as many things and promises as possible – more value;
D. To spend as little time on this as possible – more efficiency.

If you think everyone else in this transaction wants exactly the same thing as you, then you need to think again.

The first professional that you are going to meet and probably will end up spending a lot of time with is the property agent or consultant, whose role is to find you the right property or match their properties with your needs.

So what do they want? Financially, they want their commission. Emotionally, they want you to be happy with their services so that in the future, you will give them more business, either as a vendor, a buyer or as a landlord, so that financially they will have more commission. As a property sales agent, there are two ways fro them to get paid. One is that the buyer pays them, so that they represent you! They will search on the open market, see what's available there and they will do everything else for you under your instruction. The other way is that the sellers pay them (the developer or the vendor), so they will match your requirements to their stocks and see whether a successful deal can be generated. The majority of Chinese buyers at this stage are opting for the second option.

So for them, they possibly want to:

A. Make the deal happen as soon as possible
B. Make the deal go smoothly

The time urgency comes from the rule that they are paid upon completion (for second hand properties) and upon exchange of contract (for off-plan new builds).

Sellers' needs are very simple – to sell the property with highest price suitable to their time line, whether they are developers or vendors. They are selling with the goal of making a maximum profit with the minimum extra cost. As a result, they will always want to push the price as high as possible at a time line that suits their needs the best, and try to not spend any extra money on any extra request unless it is a deal breaker.

How about surveyors? You are paying them, whether they are from the bank or independently hired by you. Does that mean they are on your side? The answer is no! Surveyors' jobs are to inspect the property, report on its condition, identify any defect, make recommendations about repairs or further specialist reports and give an opinion of value. They are professionals getting paid to provide professional opinions in their field. This should not be manipulated for the user's purposes and goals. The banks will, based on the report, decide whether the property is within the risk management level for them to release the mortgage fund to you. You need to interpret the report for your own purpose to decide whether you want to buy the property or not, at the previously agreed price, or not.

How about solicitors? You pay them, so surely they should act on your behalf completely, right? The answer is "yes" and "no". "Yes" in the way that they are representing you with the solicitor that is paid by the seller and to deal with the legal process of the transfer of title for the property being sold. The object of transferring the title of land or property is to pass the freehold or leasehold right of ownership from a seller to a buyer. Simply put, their job is to get all the related legal things done so that the property will become yours. In this sense, they are representing you.

"No" in the way that they are also representing the legal systems here and they need to work with a range of other professionals such as the local council for searches and the buyers' solicitors for raising any queries. Their job is to get what they need to do done, nothing more, nothing less. You as a buyer still need to understand the procedure and make decisions based on the results and answers they have provided you with after the research.

Another important party involved is the lender; some of you might choose to go to them directly and some of you might choose to go with a mortgage broker. *"The funny thing about a bank is that they only lend money to people who don't need money"*. It is true up to a point; what they want is new business and new customers with minimum risks. The mortgage broker is getting paid mostly from the lender directly rather than from the customers, Therefore, their advantage is offering you a variety of products on the market. However, unfortunately, due to the fact that not many local banks can or are willing to lend to foreigners, your chances of finding a mortgage broker that can help you is not as high as a local buyer.

The third gap that you are facing, probably the biggest gap, is the difference between your expectations of everyone else and what everyone else has actually been doing.

Every sales agent has a list of their favorite clients and a list of their least favorite clients, and I am sure out of the professionals that you will be working with, you will also have a list of the ones that you love and the ones that you don't.

I want to share a story here with you. There was a time that I had this client – a lovely middle-aged, self-made, female millionaire with quite an impressive property portfolio in China. If I had to use three words to describe her, they would be precise, demanding and quick. She is a woman with strong power and mind; she knows what she is doing and she expects the best from everything and everyone. China is a huge country with numerous opportunities and fierce competition; she needs to have certain traits to be where she is now. The moment I took her on as a client, I knew there would be some good challenges ahead and they came sooner than I expected.

Two days after we put down the reservation fee on a high-end property, she called me. "Sally, I don't like the solicitor that you recommended me, I am going to change it, find me another one."

"Why?" I asked. The solicitors I had recommended had been working with me on quite a large number of deals and had produced great results and a group of happy clients.

"They are too slow in responding to me, and when I went to their office yesterday, she made me wait for half an hour before seeing me." She had grown impatient over the phone and her voice became louder.

"Did you make an appointment?" I asked.

"No, and why should I? I am their client." Her voice became angry.

"Why did you say they are slow in responding?" I asked again.

"I tried to call her office twice, she was not in, so I left a message with the front desk and asked her to call me back. It always took ages for her to get back to me. I cannot handle this, I expect immediate communication all the time, and especially when I am buying a property in this country. I expect to be in the picture always and clearly!"

I offered to speak to the solicitor, first, before we made any further decision, and what I got was another side of the story.

"It just happened that during the time she called me, I was either at a meeting or was out for lunch. Once I got back to my desk, I called her back straight away and I emailed her as well to follow up the conversation – with no reply from her, though. She turned up at our office asking to see me yesterday without an appointment while I was with another client discussing some issues. I understand her purchase is a rather large amount, but we treat everyone equally with all the due respect and a professional manner. We are trying our best. If she is not happy and decides to go somewhere else, although it will be a shame for us to lose a client, we will still wish her all the best."

What happened in the end? I wish I could tell you the problems were solved, yes it had been solved temporarily, but eventually, I had to find another solicitor for her... and another one after that.

She also encountered similar problems with the developer, which almost caused the deal to fall through. Luckily, I managed to pull it through; two months after the agreed contract exchange date, though.

I am not blaming anyone or pointing fingers here, unfortunately, things do turn out differently than expected sometimes due to misunderstanding, lack of communication and many existing differences.

For this particular client, I would say it was the difference between the expectation and the reality, which led her to believe that everybody else is working against her, not working with her, and she managed to turn this belief almost into reality.

The gaps that exist between you and everyone else created by all those invisible factors can be huge and daunting! Handled poorly, they can lead to damages financially, emotionally or even cause the deal to fall through completely.

So how to handle the differences, stay on top of everything and everyone else with minimum effort and hassle?

> *"We all do better when we work together. Our differences do matter, but our common humanity matters more."*
> *- Bill Clinton*

Well, there is no need to bring in common humanity here, but you get the idea right? "Find the common ground among all the differences" is the key I am giving you here in this chapter; I will also teach you a few skills to help you use this key. In no time, you will find this will be the easiest part of the whole buying process.

So what is the common ground?

Simple: To have a deal and to have the deal done!

Without a deal, there is no existence for the surveyor; without a done deal, the agent will not get his/her commission, the developer or the seller will not be able to sell the product and count their profit, the solicitor will not get their full fee in place and the lenders will not have you as their long term client.

So, for everyone at least to have the potential to be happy is to have a deal and have this deal done.

With this simple fact in mind, you will perceive everyone with a different perspective; they are there to help you, work for you, and assist you in achieving this common goal. You are the leader to give that little push when needed with these great skills.

Skill one: use your charming communication skills. I believe that anyone who can afford to buy a property in a foreign country has this in them, although sometimes the pressure of not speaking the language gets in the way and they forget about this skill that they have.

If language is your main problem, then find an agent who speaks your language and lead him/her with your charm.

Communication is the key in almost all the relationships, and the one between yourself and your agent is exceptionally important – especially when you choose this role to be your prime contact and communication point. Keep it going at all costs; even if things start to get a little strained because things are not moving along quite as quickly as you would like them to, keep the lines of contact open. It is in nobody's interest to let the communication break down. You have a property to buy and they have a commission to make.

Make your contact point simple: one person per role, ideally. You will most likely find that other people in the same office know little about your sale and communication will be more efficient and less frustrating if it is all conducted with a single person. Which means one person from the agent, one person in the solicitor firm, one person from the lender, etc.

Keep your communication efficient, timely and try not to over communicate. Phoning up the agent or the solicitor or the bank every day is not going to make things faster or put you on the top of their list, nor is it going to help the sale go through any quicker. Although you are the boss here and your prime goal is not to win the popularity vote and become friends with everyone, it does no harm to try and stay on the good side of the professional people you are working with throughout the deal.

Try to avoid visiting their premises unless it's absolutely necessary. Nowadays, we can get things done without even meeting the clients thanks to the invention of telephone, fax machine, post and internet, etc. If you do need to speak to someone or to meet up, make an appointment first. You would be annoyed if your solicitor was concentrating on your case and someone without an appointment walked in and disturbed him/her; nor would you like to be disturbed while in the middle of something yourself, right? So there is no reason to expect that your agent, solicitor, developer or lender will be available to see you or speak to you on the spur of the moment. Making an appointment also helps make sure that they have the information you require at hand when you do drop in.

There is an invisible but most common communication rule in the UK property industry: **Put everything in writing** if you can, especially important stages of the sales – offer accepted, solicitor appointed, purchase price agreed, additional requirements required, etc. "Black and white", as we say. You should also write to them if any of your circumstances change, so if something happens, you at least will have the proof to cover your own back. For instance, one of my recent deals involved a rather prolonged price negotiation process with the developer; in the end, the offer for discount came in a package of a variety of things, such as a free furniture pack, a small amount of discount on the purchase price, and a £1,000 contribution from the developer towards the solicitor fee. However, this contribution was negotiated after the reservation form was filled and filed. Which means it was not written in the initial reservation form. Instead, the developer offered it some time into the legal process, with a condition that this would only come into place upon completion, which is in two years' time from now. See, things like this MUST be communicated and kept in email/written format by the clients, the agent and the solicitor. What if in two years' time, the person from the developer has changed his/her job?

Skill two: have the right attitude and manage your expectations.

"If you don't like something, change it. If you can't change it, change your attitude. Don't complain." I love this quote by Maya Angelou, and it applies to all areas in life, including your property buying experience in a foreign country.

As much as you want the other person to change, maybe you want the solicitor to answer your calls 24/7, or you want the bank to tell you straight away that you can get the loan. You want the developer to give you a great discount and a great number of freebies, to value you as a long-term great client with potential to introduce more buyers. If they don't behave the way you expected, instead of getting frustrated, change your attitude, show some appreciation and manage your expectations. You have more chances to win this way.

Try to build an open and honest relationship with your agent first; if everyone always knows where he or she stands, it is much easier to work together to achieve a common goal. Of course, this applies as well to your agent but you must do your share.

Yes, it is true that buyers are from Mars and everyone else is from Venus. However, you will still go a long way if you understand and respect the differences and pull out your bags of charms.

Chapter Seven
The Great Expectations -
Steps, Procedures and Timelines

Have you ever played a computer game with a child? Perhaps, you bought them a Playstation for their birthday along with a classic game - Super Mario. The kid then got hooked on it and played whenever he had a chance. Two months later, he invited you to play with him on a sunny Sunday afternoon. You happened to be free, needed to unwind anyway, so you sat down with him and thought, "How hard could this be?" You have heard of this game and you have watched him playing a couple of times. He is only 7 years old, wears thick glasses and you are a grown, mature, intelligent, independent professional businessman who owns a company with over 100 employees.

So you took over the controller and started; you knew that you needed to collect coins, avoid falling to your death or getting killed by a flower with teeth. You cleared the first level with great care and accidentally jumped just a tiny bit too far into the death trap in order to avoid the unexpected movement of a turtle and you died. "Not too bad," you thought to yourself as you started to visualise the ways to avoid making the same mistake next time it was your turn. You handed the controller to the 7-year-old kid. Oh, boy, did you ever expect this? He was flying, he collected a lot more coins than you, got himself some treasures to fly, shoot, grow bigger and avoid traps that you could not even see properly. He was on fire. Half an hour later, you got the controller again, the pressure was on, you made it to five minutes long this time with some sweat and passed the controller back to the 7-year-old kid reluctantly and waited for another half an hour or so for your next turn. And this went on for the whole afternoon until the moment you couldn't take it anymore and ended everything with your grown-up's authority.

Has this ever happened to you? If not, go and play a computer game with a young kid and I almost guarantee you a similar experience.

So, why can a kid that is so much younger than you, shorter than you, less experienced than you, poorer than you, beat you so badly in a computer game?

You know the answer for sure! And yes, you are right! He has played the game before, and in the above case, he has played the game whenever he has had a chance for the past two months! He probably read a couple of books on how to pass the difficult levels, watched a few YouTube tutorials, and played with his friends a few times while you were at work.

The key is he knew what to expect! And that gave him the power.

And this is the power I want you to have in buying a property in the UK, or any foreign country – "Know what to expect!" so that you can "ANTICIPATE"!

Do you still remember the powerful young couple that I mentioned in the previous chapter? The husband said how useless and helpless he felt, and how he felt he was deaf and mute because he could not speak the language? Imagine how frustrated he must have felt once the legal process started? After they put down the deposit to their dream home in the UK? To find the property in the first place suddenly seemed to be such a simple task. Although they couldn't speak the language or understand it, the house, as a physical object, is there for them to see, feel and touch. Then the beginning of the legal process threw them right into the DARK AGES, without any clue of what to expect, who to expect or how long to expect.

This chapter is designed to answer those questions in a simple, easy-to-understand way to give you the power of "anticipation".

Let's say that you have put down the reservation fee, done the reservation form and informed your acting solicitors: **What to EXPECT Next?**

The good news is that you and your agents have just lifted a heavy task off your shoulders, now the great expectations are passed onto the solicitors from both parties.

Your solicitor will usually send you a confirmation email and/or letter to confirm your instructions, along with an estimated price quotation for the whole process, including the stamp duty and their legal fee, etc.

In the meantime, after the seller's solicitor confirms their instructions with the seller, both of them need to get to work straight away. The seller's solicitor needs to start gathering information, collecting the title deeds/official copies, preparing a draft contract and asking the seller to fill in the fittings and contents form.

Once these are done, they will send them to your solicitor together with the draft contract. Upon receiving this, your solicitor will send the local search to the local authority and any specialist searches.

There are things you may not know about the property just from viewing it with your agent or even the survey report. The solicitor will do a set of legal searches to ensure there are no other factors you should be aware of. Things like whether there are plans for a motorway in your new back garden, whether there is flood risk to your new property (the fact that your property is not sitting on a riverbank does not necessarily mean the area your property is in will be flood-proof), whether you will receive an unexpected huge bill from a local church, which is two blocks away from your new property, that needs repair in the future, how you are going to get your water and if any public drains on the property might affect extensions or building works, whether there is a chance for a local farmer to herd his sheep across your land if you are buying a massive country house with acres of land attached to it (and generally speaking, whether other people have access to part of your property).

This procedure usually takes a lot of time and neither you nor the solicitor can fully control it, as it is dependent on the speed of the local authority that your new property belongs to; the difference ranges from 1-2 weeks to around 6 weeks.

Your solicitor will also need to carefully examine the draft contract and supporting documents and raise enquiries with the sellers' solicitors. You will be expected to go through the forms the seller has completed and let the solicitor know if you have any queries or concerns too. Things you should pay particular attention to are the tenure of your new home: is it leasehold or freehold, as you were told before? If leasehold, double check the length of the lease, was it the same as what you were told initially? Are the spelling of your name and other personal details on the draft contract correct? Are all the pre-agreed terms written in the contract? Don't just rely on the solicitors to do this! Your solicitor will also raise some questions upon receiving the draft contract, so make sure you give enough attention to him/her at this stage and build up a clear and open communication so that you know why your solicitor was asking the questions he/she asked, what his/her concern was and what the answers would mean to you.

Again, if you are using an English solicitor and if they don't have a Chinese speaking person in that office, go back to your agent and ask for help. Don't worry, they will help you!! Remember? They won't get their commission unless the deal is complete.

Alternatively, you can use some professional translation services or simply a Chinese solicitor firm.

The length of this stage depends on the questions that have been raised and the speed of responding. Sometimes there will be a few rounds of question-and-answer time. You do not want to rush this, as you want to get all the questions cleared out of the way and be absolutely comfortable with all the answers that you will be getting. However, there is no harm in pushing the seller and the solicitors a little to ensure that they are on schedule with this.

While this is happening, if you are buying a second hand property, you will also be busy looking at the surveyor reports to see whether further actions need to be taken.

Two things require your full attention and action here: firstly, your deposit should also be arranged and ready to go any time, especially when you are an international buyer. Once you and your solicitor are happy with all the answers and research, you will need to transfer the agreed deposit to your solicitor's account before he/she can arrange the exchange of contract. So if you are from overseas, you need to arrange this in a timely manner to avoid any delay (remember, there is a good chance you will be fined if you failed to exchange the contract within a certain period of time with new build development.)

Secondly, you need to decide on a building insurance policy, especially for a second hand property. Big commitment comes with big responsibilities and the property will become your responsibility the moment the contract is exchanged. For new developments, it usually comes with a warranty of up to 10 years.

Now, with all the research reports back, questions all answered and satisfied, survey done (optional), deposit with your solicitor, contract signed by both the buyer and the seller – it is time to exchange the contract with an agreed completion date set.

For a new build off-plan development, it usually takes 28 days for the contract to be exchanged and it will take up to 3 months or even longer for a second hand property.

In the UK property buying process, exchange of contract is like a marriage registration in a relationship. This is the point when everything becomes serious! Before this point, both you and the seller were only trying to work out something together, without any guarantee, and either party could walk out of it at any time without any penalty. Just like in a boyfriend-girlfriend relationship, you can just get up and leave without any serious consequences, or even without the need to give the other party a clear explanation or true explanation. It could be you have found someone that is more suitable for you, or you found out some ugly truth about the other person and did not want to go any further before it became too late, or simply because you got cold feet and were not ready for a relationship. Whatever you have spent for the dates, such as a nice meal out, little trips together, you would not expect to recoup, right?

Same thing here before you exchange the contract; you can terminate the progress any time. It could be the survey report shows that the property has Japanese knotweed and you don't have any money to deal with it; it could be you have found a nicer property with cheaper price; it could be your circumstances have changed and you are not in a position to buy anymore. Whatever the reason, you can walk away from it. And usually, you can't expect the solicitor and other parties to refund you the money you have already spent (unless pre-agreed). Vice versa, your seller can change his/her mind too.

Everything changes once the exchange of contract takes place. Things will become quite serious as both of the parties are legally bound to commit. If not, there will be money loss or even a lawsuit. For you as a buyer, if you change your mind, or your changed circumstances force you to get out of it, then you will most likely lose the deposit you have already paid, plus possibility of a further fine and a chance to be sued by the seller.

Unlike most other contracts, a contract for the sale of property must be in writing, must be signed by both parties and must contain all of the agreed terms. To comply with these formalities, the parties' solicitors will formally exchange each part of the contract: one copy signed by the seller and one copy signed by you, the buyer. Together they form the binding contract.

Many years ago, the solicitors for the seller and buyer would meet and actually exchange contracts in identical form signed by their respective clients. This does not happen today and the solicitors usually agree to the exchange over the telephone, using a standard set of "undertakings".

Reaching the exchange of contracts is the difficult part – after that it should be relatively smooth sailing. The next big step is completion – when you take possession of the property and can move in. But before that, there are things you and the solicitors need to do.

There are plenty of things to keep you busy here; first of all, you need to transfer the balance of the price list you received from your solicitor to his/her company account. Secondly, you may want to inform the utility companies and local council that it is your property. Thirdly, if you bought the property for self-use, then you should start to arrange the post re-direction and inform all the related parties of your change of address.

In the meantime, the solicitors are also working towards the agreed completion date, which should be written into the contract. It usually takes between 7 to 28 days for a second hand property from the exchange of contract to completion but it can take up to 2 to 3 years for an off-plan unit if that's the time for it to be built; obviously, no one can do a completion before the property is completed, right?! The seller's solicitor will send evidence of title to your solicitor for him/her to check the seller's title to the property. If you have a mortgage arrangement, this is the time for your solicitor to also check if your mortgage money is available, send a draft transfer, ask you to sign some final documents and then forward these to the seller's solicitor for them to check the mortgage redemption figure, approve the draft transfer, calculate the completion monies and obtain title deeds.

Once your solicitor receives the title deeds and has done the final searches, good news: you will receive a notice informing you that "both parties are now at a position for completion".

Congratulations! You have gone a long way, from the moment that you decided to purchase a property in the UK, the soul searching, the market research, the frustration, the money arrangement, the ups and downs, now the final moment is here and you have got an actual date. What do you do? What should you expect on the completion day?

Your solicitor will transfer the money to the seller's solicitor and collect the remaining title deeds. Then your solicitor needs to pay stamp duty land tax for you, register the transfer in your name and send title deeds to your lender or you; whereas the seller's solicitor is busy working on the final settlement of the seller's mortgage account and other amounts. Completion takes place when the solicitor receives money. Funds are sent through the banking system, so it is impossible to speed up after they have been sent. It can sometimes take a few hours to move through the system. It is important to remember that the contractual completion time is usually 1pm or even later, so you may not be able to move before then. Once the seller's solicitor has received the money, he/she will contact your solicitor and agent to advise that the keys can be released.

Then it's the time for you to open that bottle of champagne and celebrate!

Seller's Solicitor	Buyer's Solicitor	You the buyer
Obtains title deeds/official copies, prepares draft contract; obtains replies to PIF and fittings and contents form	Confirms instructions and gathers information. Receives and checks draft contract and other documentation	Pay attention to search report, draft contract, solicitor's enquiries, get the deposit transferred to your solicitor's bank account and find the insurance for your new property
Receives further enquiries, completes with seller and returns to buyer's solicitor	Sends local search to local authority and any specialist searches	
Receives further enquiries, completes with seller and returns to buyer's solicitor	Sends out any further enquiries to clarify points on PIF etc.	

Engrossed contract prepared

Contract signed by the seller	Contract signed by the buyer and deposit paid	

Engrossed Contracts (Contract now legally binding on buyer and seller) Completion date set.

Sends evidence of title to buyer's solicitor	Checks seller's title to property	Transfer remaining balance to the solicitor account
Checks mortgage redemption figure, approves draft transfer, calculate completion monies	Checks buyer's mortgage money is available, sends draft transfer, buyer signs final documents	Inform utility companies and local council, post redirection and all that need to know your change of address

Completion (The day the transfer is finalised and all monies paid over)

Receives purchase money and hands over keys to buyer	Hands over purchase money and collects remaining title deeds	
Final settlement of seller's mortgage account and other amounts	Pays stamp duty land tax, registers transfer in buyer's name, sends title deeds to buyer's lender or buyer	

Now you know what to expect in a normal transaction, but what if things go wrong, unexpected things happen, what do you need to do? How do you handle them?

Not to worry, I am going to show you **how to expect the unexpected too!**

Unexpected scenario 1: Your lender's survey report is back with a valuation of £800,000, which is £200,000 lower than the agreed purchase price of £1 million. Initially the bank agreed to lend you £600,000, now they are only agreeing to lend you £480,000. So what are you going to do?

You have two options here, buy the property at £1 million, put down £520,000 from your own pocket and take the £480,000. Would you do that? The answer is probably no. If the bank only valuates the property at £800,000, which means you are buying a property that is overpriced based on the bank valuation, you need to think about what happens if you want to resell it in the future; will you be able to make some profit or even cover your cost?

So what are you going to do in a situation like this? Are you going to walk away from this once and for all? To start the search all over again can be daunting, plus there is already some cost involved up till now. Are you going to go ahead buying it regardless of the risks because you just love the property so much that you must have it?

My suggestion would be: Contact your agent and ask for help. A good agent should be able to actively find a solution for you. The agent should ask the bank for the valuation report and the reasons for the downward valuation. Then your agent should contact the seller again and ask for a further price reduction to reflect the valuation report. After all, if the bank you used was a major bank, then there is a high chance another potential buyer will face a similar valuation report, and the seller will possibly face the same situation again in the future if they let you go. Use the reasons for the downward valuation, as your arguing points and you will stand a good chance of winning this. Otherwise, if you do have to walk away, then walk away. You know that you will lose the occuring costs, such as the solicitor fee and survey fee, but we are talking about a difference of a couple of thousand pounds and £200K here; the decision should not be too difficult to make.

Scenario 2: What if just days before exchange of contract, the seller informs you that he/she is going to increase the purchase price by £5,000 from £550,000 to £555,000. Can he/she do that? What should you do if this happens?

Well, unfortunately, this does happen and there is no law against this sort of behaviour, yet. If supply is shorter than demand and the property price is rising quickly, and the seller wants to get some extra money for it, he/she can. Sometimes they do it when there is another buyer offering to pay more, and sometimes, they do it just to try without even having another buyer in the picture.

So what should you do if this unfortunate situation happens to you at the last minute before the exchange of contract? I would suggest that you contact your solicitor or your agent (this again stresses the importance of finding a good, trustworthy and competent agent) to help you to negotiate with the seller and see what happens. At the end of the day, the decision is yours, some buyers take this move as a sign of greed and unreliability, they will just walk away, straight away, without even trying as they have lost faith in the seller. Others have a bottom line of how much extra they can pay for and will try to see whether that's achievable at this stage.

What else can you do to prevent this? Well, there are certain things you can do which will help a bit, remember the rules of "written" communication records I mentioned before? That everything needs to be "black and white" to cover your back? The moment that you have got an agreed purchase price and filled in the reservation form, email or write to the seller's agent or the developer that you want them to remove the property from the market immediately (you need to orally discuss this with them before you put down the offer). You should check yourself, as well, to see if the property was, in fact, removed. By doing so, you are decreasing the chance for other buyers to see this property and potentially put down a higher offer, especially in the sellers' market when the supply is lower than the demand. If you can, also put down a term of agreed purchase price without any increase before exchange of contract.

Scenario 3: Usually it is 7-28 days between the exchange of contract and completion. However, your seller has disagreed with that and said well in advance that due to their personal circumstances, they want exchange and completion on the same day. Is this OK for you? Should you do it? And if so, what should you pay attention to?

First of all, don't panic. A lot of times, this is a good situation for you the buyer as it certainly can speed things up, especially when you are a cash buyer and there are no chains either from the seller's side or from your side. Two things you need to pay attention to: one, if you or the seller has a chain, which means either you need to sell a property to get the money, or the seller needs to complete a deal on buying a new property before moving out of the one you want to buy, it generally creates more complications when more people get involved, which means everyone on the chain needs to work out a time line that can make this happen. Two, the money! If you are a cash buyer, then you are fine. If not, some of the lenders are OK with exchange and completion on the same day, others are not; instead they probably will ask for a few days' notice in advance for them to get the money ready. If this is the case you need to get the money situation straightened out beforehand to make things happen.

Scenario 4: You were told the completion day would be on Wednesday, the 1st of May, you have got all the furniture deliveries arranged for that day in the early afternoon, however, you received no call before lunchtime informing you to go and pick up keys. Then you waited till 3 o'clock in the afternoon and were told it was not going to happen that day, and you would have to wait until tomorrow. Is this even possible?

The answer is yes, unfortunately! Although, it rarely happens. Do you remember earlier on, I told you that the completion only happens when the seller's solicitor receives the money and the money is transferred via the banking system and once it is transferred, it is impossible to push it or to speed it up? Unfortunate things can happen, such as there is a fault with the banking system, or you have a chain of transaction and one of the chains gets stuck; or the mortgage money does not arrive on time. No matter how much notice your solicitor gives your mortgage lender, they will never guarantee when the money will arrive in their account. The problem arises because the banking system shuts down for telegraphic transfer after 3 pm. So if your mortgage money doesn't arrive until 4:45, then it is just too late to do anything with it except wait for the next day.

When things like this happen, there is not much you can do except wait patiently. So do not be too eager and book all the furniture deliveries on the completion day, just in case.

Scenario 5: Your solicitor has told you that everything is almost ready and you should transfer the money to them and get ready for exchange and completion, however, the money has been returned a couple of times without reaching the seller's account. What's happening? And what can you do?

As peculiar as it sounds, it can really happen. A friend of mine went through this unpleasant experience not long ago unfortunately. What happens is that if two people initially signed the title deed, then you need both of their signatures on the paper when it comes to sales. However, things change, and if the couple go separate ways, it can become a problem to get both of them to sign; the worst situation is that one of them refuses to sign.

When things happen like this, what can you do? Not much! You cannot force them to sign, neither can your solicitor, all you can do is just wait and wish yourself luck. My friend got lucky and completed the deal finally, but for you, pay a bit attention and know where you stand; prepare for it would be my advice.

Those are some of the common situations that you would not normally expect. However, every transaction and every property is different, I am sure that one day you probably will experience something that is not even described here, so how do you deal with things that are even beyond these?

Remember the simple rules: stay calm, look into the situation again, identify what is the problem, reconfirm your own bottom line, go back to your trusted agent for help, go back to the solicitor for help, and that will give you a pretty good start!

Chapter Eight
How to Stay Sane

When I bought my first property in the UK years ago, my mum became crazily scared and unsure. I just got my work permit, was single, lived in a shared house with two housemates and was not on a good salary. My plan back then was simple: to buy a small place outside London, rent it out, use the rental income from the place to cover most of my rental expenses in London, save up most of my salary till I was done with my work permit, find a better job with a better salary and buy another property in London for myself to live in. I chose to buy outside London at that time simply because I could not afford a piece of London. I had a small deposit and the bank wouldn't lend me much money.

As scared as she was, my mum still tried her best to be supportive of me, and my dad had exhausted all his tricks to keep her sane and get the sleep she needed during that three months.

I remember that on the day when I finally got the keys to that flat, I took a picture of me turning the key in the front door and sent it the my mum, and that was the moment she finally believed that everything was fine and I owned the property.

Years later, when I started to help overseas buyers (mainly Chinese) purchase a property in the UK, I started to meet so many mums and dads who reminded me of my own parents. A lot of them are buying for their kids who are even younger than I was back then, which means the parents have to take on all the pressure and stress themselves. Many of them deal with stress pretty well and many of them don't; quite a few of them let the fear, stress and emotion cloud their minds and turn the property buying process into a big, traumatic, unpleasant experience.

And this is one of the reasons I wanted to write this book, not only to help the buyers to understand the systems here, to have the power of anticipation, but also to create for them a rather fun, interesting and productive experience while making one of the biggest financial decisions in their lives.

In this chapter, I will teach you how to stay sane while buying a piece of the UK with your money. And I want to start this process by exploring seven concerns that drive buyers to insanity.

Concern One:
Not knowing the exit strategy

When I started writing this book, I called my mum and asked her the question that I had not thought of asking in the past years: "Mum, remember that time when I said I was going to buy that flat in the UK, and you went really quiet and not sure? What was your concern? What was the thought that kept you awake at night?"

I thought she would say things like, you were too young, you never bought a property before, or you didn't know the system, or maybe you were single, why not wait till you met someone. But guess what? Her answer was something that I did not expect; rather than worrying about my ability to buy it, she was actually thinking way ahead of me.

"You just got your work permit and no one knows what kind of changes the immigration policy will undergo in five years' time. Will you be able to continue to stay in the UK or not? Will you want to stay there five years from now? After you bought that property, what if you were not in the UK any more, we don't have any family or close friends there, what will happen to that flat? The money will be tied down there, and if you want to sell it, how? And if you do manage to sell it, how do you get the money back, because by that time we will all be in China? That was my worry!"

She was worried about the "exit" strategy, if things went sour in the future. And for all these years, I had never thought of it because I had never asked her. How bad the communication between parents and kids can be, even for the closest relationship in the world!

That's the reason I have been stressing the skills and needs of communication. It is important that you need to understand for yourself the product, the market and the people that you are going to work with first, but it is also crucial for you to clearly communicate what is in your head to the professionals that you will be working with so that they know what you want! The better you communicate, the higher chance that you will get your desired result.

If you have similar thoughts like my mum had and this thought keeps you up at night, worries you and drives you crazy, then you should continue reading.

Let's say something unwanted happens in the future,

or simply changed circumstances made you unable to visit or stay in this country and you have a property here that's quite a big asset. What can you do?

First of all, you DO HAVE the options of either selling it or letting it and finding a management company to manage it for you during your absence. I will talk about this more in detail in the last chapter of this book on the cost of selling, cost of letting and management, etc. But the point is you will HAVE the options.

Secondly, the money will be yours, whether it is the rental income or it's the sales figure. There will be some procedures, some deductions, but you will get the money.

After all, some of the reasons that people are investing or buying in the UK property market is because of the stable political environment, the well-established legal system and well-regulated property services industry.

So, the good news is that yes, there is an exit strategy for you.

Concern Two:
Not being able to find the right property

I have to say that there have been quite a few times I came across buyers that were so frustrated and tired and exhausted from the property search that they were ready to give up once and for all. They had been searching for quite a while and just could not find the right property.

Yes, buying a property is not like buying a Chinese lettuce, it is expensive and it is a big commitment and things could go wrong if you are not careful. But dragging it on for an unnecessary amount of time while you could use this time to do something that is more valuable and meaningful also makes no sense, wouldn't you agree?

There are some simple steps that will help you to shorten the search period.

Step One: back to the basics, go through chapter one of this book "It's All About You" and figure out why you want to buy in the first place. If you are buying for investment, then it should be an easier decision. If you are buying for self-use, write down your requirements on a piece of paper, and rank them based on their importance to you.

Step Two: know what you can afford to get. Figure out all the financial stuff as I mentioned before in chapter five, "Money, Money, Money".

Step Three: communicate with your chosen agent and make sure you communicate well.

Step Four: send your agent to work and look at the options he/she has for you, give necessary feedback each time to improve the search.

Step Five: manage your emotions and expectations. If you are looking for an investment property, then you do not need to love it, although make sure you don't hate it either. If you are searching for a self-use property, remember, it is very rare that people will get 100% of what they want, so consider a property that can offer you most of the things at the top of your wanting list and learn to see the potentials.

Keep your eyes open, goals clear and stay focused!

Concern Three:
What if people leave us before the completion date?

I met a couple at an exhibition last time I was in Shanghai and they remained one of my favourite clients ever since. They were very polite, well-spoken, gentle and low key. They wanted to buy a flat for their son in London when he graduated from the university in a year's time so that the son would not need to throw away money on rent. Instead he could start his life in the UK by living in a rather decent flat of his own and use the money for rent on mortgage repayments. In their words, "You take out money from your left pocket and put it back into your right pocket."

The wife was very quiet and shy but with a good head on her shoulders; she reminded me so much of my mother. The husband was cautious at the beginning, asking me a lot of questions that I was pretty sure he knew the answers to himself but asked anyway just to test out my knowledge of the UK property market. After I passed his test, he offered me his complete trust. From that moment forwards, I worked my socks off just to repay the respect and trust he offered to me so generously.

Their plan was to get their financial matters sorted in China while I was here in the UK narrowing down the research and squeezing out all the best options for them to view in one day, two months from our initial meeting in China.

And they wanted to be able to make a decision on that short trip to London. The pressure was on; to fail this was to fail their expectations and their trust in me. You can imagine how stressed I was during those two months.

Luckily, thanks to clear communication and thorough preparation from their end, we managed to pull it off and they put down the reservation fee for an off-plan new build apartment in the Greenwich area on that very day. I was so relieved and happy that it was an immediate mutual decision among the family of three. They seemed to me very happy.

Then the wife said something to me on our way to the ladies: "Sally, what if in a few months' time, you make a life changing decision and change your career or you move to another country, what's going to happen to us and our property? Are we still going to be able to complete it in two years' time as the completion date for this site is two years from now? Is the property still going to be ours?" She looked very shy after she asked this question; a look on her face showed me that she was reluctant to question me, but the concern must have been really bothering her for her, to speak out loud and confront me face to face.

If you have similar concerns and worries, don't feel afraid, speak it out, and talk to your agent or the professionals that are going to help you in the process. "Don't ask, don't get"; you need to know what you are getting yourself into from the very beginning, to clear your concerns and worries in order to be able to enjoy this journey rather than staying up at night for the most part.

The answer to this question is YES, you can still buy the property.

If during your buying process, one of the professionals that you have been working with decided to quit their job or became unavailable, stay calm, it's not the end of the world and there are solutions.

Your agent's role mainly is to help you find the right property, start the process and monitor it for you. Once you pass on the solicitor's details to the agent and the seller, it will then be the solicitor's major job to get all the legal work done. The agent's existence is to make things easier but the lack of their existence is not going to kill it. However, do make sure that you keep the written record of the important things that your agent mentioned to you to avoid dispute in the future.

If your solicitor decided to quit or personal circumstances forced him/her to become unavailable to handle your case, then, before that happens, usually the firm will arrange another person to take up the responsibilities, but you do still need to make sure you keep a written record of the important things. Or if you want to change solicitor firm, you can give instructions to your new chosen solicitor firm, and they will do the transfer for you.

What if the developer has gone bankrupt in two years' time? Unfortunately, this is just one of the risks that you need to face when you are buying an off-plan unit, anywhere in the world. However, in the UK, do your research and you will cut down the risk to a minimum level. First of all, do research on the developer of the sites, and talk to your agent and see whether there is anything in particular that could lead to any suspicion. Secondly, if you can, ask your agent to arrange a viewing for you to their site's sales and marketing suite to have a look at the quality of their finished products. Thirdly, do research on the UK property industry's regulatory bodies to have a basic idea of how the industry works and what you could do to protect yourself if something does go wrong. For instance, you should familiarise yourself with this term "NHBC warranty" at least. NHBC is the UK's leading standard-setting body and provider of warranty and insurance for new homes. Their role is to work with the house-building industry to raise the standards of new homes and to provide consumer protection for homebuyers. Currently, 80% of new homes in the UK come with a 10-year warranty under this National House-Building Council (NHBC) scheme.

For more information, you can log on to their website: www.nhbc.co.uk.

Concern Four:
How can I trust people with my money?

Put another way, how do you know you have not been involved in a scam and given away your money to some stranger?

This had never been an issue until one of my previous clients expressed his concern in an email, trying very hard not to make it sound rude.

Here is the story: I found him a property to buy, the client went back to China, did all the paper work very efficiently and then it came time for the solicitor to send him the bill. They asked him to transfer 10% of the deposit to the solicitor's account so that she could get ready for the exchange, shortly. He became very worried. The solicitor cc'd me in every email because the client didn't speak English and the solicitor didn't speak Chinese. The next morning, I got an email from the client directly, without a cc to the solicitor:

"Sally, shall we transfer the money? If so, why not to the developer's account instead to the solicitor's account? What if the solicitor takes the money and runs? We are truly worried, and we need your help!"

I always tell my clients from the very beginning that in the UK, the property buying process, with its own system and rules, is rather different than in China and many other countries in the world. Here, both buyer and seller need a solicitor (generally speaking, unless you can handle all the conveying process by yourself without using a solicitor), and the buyer needs to transfer the money to the solicitor's account for exchange and for completion. Then the buyer's solicitor will transfer the money to the seller's solicitor before they pass on the money to the seller afterwards. So you see, there is generally no direct money contact between the buyer and the seller.

But for some reason, this client and many of my other clients sometimes don't register this information, and when the time comes to transfer the money, they get worried, they think it is a trap, that the seller will never see the money and the third party will take the money and go.

As I mentioned many times before, one of the reasons that international investors like to buy properties in the UK is because of its well-established legal system and well-regulated property industry.

Just make sure you have done your research properly on the solicitor firm you will be using, keep the communication open and effective, and you will do just fine.

Concern Five:
How do I know that I own the property?

In China, you will get a "property ownership certificate" after you've bought a property; it is a little red booklet, the size of a passport.

Many of my buyers will expect to receive one of these as well upon completion of the property, and they got frustrated and disbelieving that if they don't get one.

My mum was one of them. For her, I think the picture of me turning the key in the front door lock kind of put her concern to ease. To her, true ownership means either you have the red certificate or you have the keys to the property.

So, what's the system here? How do you know you are the owner of the property other than receiving the keys on the completion day and being told by your solicitor and your agent – "this property is yours"?

The answer is "land registry".

One of your solicitor's jobs is to prepare a summary of the document transferring ownership to you and register your details as the new owner with the land registry system, which usually will be completed around a month after the completion of your property. The land registry has a file for every piece of land registered there and on that file your ownership is recorded. It is public information and can be accessed online.

Concern Six:
What if the property is crap and something is horribly wrong with it that I don't know?

If this is the one biggest problem that keeps you awake at night, I would suggest you go back and re-read chapter two, "It's All About the Property Too" and chapter seven, "The Great Expectations" and you will find the answers there.

Generally speaking, there are four steps for you to minimise the risk without nasty surprises in the future.

Step 1: equip yourself with all the necessary knowledge about the various types of properties, especially the traits of the type of property you are thinking of buying. This will help you look for the right clues that will lead to potential deal breaker faults of the property during your viewing.

Step 2: read the bank's valuation report for any suspicious clues and comments. However, this step only applies to a property that requires mortgage arrangement.

Step 3: read surveyor's report for any suspicious clues and comments. Ask if you don't understand the terms or if the valuation is lower than the asking price, and find out the reason behind the surveyor's decision.

Step 4: pay attention to your solicitor's raised enquiries and the seller's answers, as this process will disclose a lot of matters that you won't be able to tell purely from property viewing or even the surveyor reports.

Remember the metaphor of the boyfriend-girlfriend relationship VS marriage? You can walk away any time before the exchange of the contract or ask for a re-negotiation of the purchase price if you find something that would be of any big concern to you.

Do this right; you should not put yourself in the position of finding skeletons in the closet in the future.

Concern Seven:
Worry about the deal falling through

A good friend of mine who has never bought a property in the UK, went through a short period of insomniac nights before his first property here was exchanged a couple of years ago.

He started his own property search calmly and in a very organized way; he spent a couple of months in finding the right property for him at the time, made the reservation, got the mortgage and solicitor both in place straight after the reservation. Everything went fine, and yet suddenly, for some reason, he went from super calm to super anxious, and he lost his ability to sleep a couple of weeks before the exchange of contract. Thankfully, the exchange went smoothly and on schedule, otherwise, I truly doubt how long he could have kept his sanity before he completely lost it.

I was not involved in the transaction and so did not ask him any questions back then. Once he found out about this book, especially this chapter, he offered his side of the story hoping that the sharing of his experience could help many other buyers.

"I worried that the deal would fall through at the last minute," he confessed. "I knew I had done everything I could from my side, but I don't know that much about buying a property here in the UK; most of my friends and colleagues were either relocated here or they don't own a property here. So, I was getting most of my information from various websites without a complete picture of what to expect. My solicitor and agent were in touch with me at the beginning of the process asking for different documents and information, but after that, they went quiet on me for a while. I felt I was kept in the dark. Then I read an article online saying that a large number of deals don't get to the stage of exchange. That was the point I went crazy and I could not sleep any more. What made me feel even worse was the fact that it was all out of my control, there was nothing I could do to change anything… luckily, it all went really well."

If what I have just described here represents your fear, then go back to chapter seven, "The Great Expectations", and equip yourself with the power of "anticipation"! Once you have a clear idea of what to expect, who to expect, when to expect, you will feel much better and it will be easy for you to rise to another level and stay on top of everything. Even the unexpected deal-falling-through situation.

After all, buying a property in the UK or any country is a financial activity that comes with risks; you need to be emotionally and financially prepared for it.

I am sure there will be a lot of other reasons to drive a lot of our buyers insane during the process. The general rule is don't get upset, look at the problem first, know your bottom line, communicate with your agent or solicitor or any other professionals who can help you, find out more about the problem and see what you can do about it.

At the end of the day, buying a property is not a life and death issue, so try to take it easy.

Part Three

Party Afterwards?

Chapter Nine
What Next?

So, now you have got the keys, you officially and legally own a piece of the UK. Congratulations! You made it.

What next? Open up a few bottles of champagne, invite some friends along, get to know your neighbours and throw a party?

Yes, yes, you can do all that and you absolutely deserve it. But in the meanwhile, let's keep it real and get you to do a little more work before complete relaxation.

I promise I will keep this chapter short and sweet so that you have time to organise that party!

First things first, **keep in touch with your solicitor**. I always joke with my friends that you definitely get your money's worth with a good solicitor because they will still be working for you even after you get the keys. A lot of buyers think that the solicitors' work is done upon completion and they are so wrong.

There are still a few things they need to do, quite important things actually. One of them is that they need to complete and file the stamp duty land tax (SDLT) return form to the tax man (HM Revenue & Customs) and pay the money; the other thing is they need to tie up the loose ends on matters regarding your mortgage and insurance; last but not least, they need to get you that "property ownership certificate" (in our Chinese terms). Your solicitor will do all the work and communicate with the related departments in the land registry to ensure the transfer of the registration is complete. Once your solicitor receives the title information document showing the new title entries, he/she needs to check everything to make sure that your names are correctly spelled as the new registered owner, any mortgage has been properly registered and any previous mortgages have been removed from the register if that's the case.

By the time all of this is done, you may receive a bundle of documents again relating to the property; this could happen a few weeks after you get your key. Make sure you keep them safe because you might need to refer to them in the future, especially when you decide to sell it on. When that time comes, it will save you time and money if you hand these documents to your solicitor.

Next, **let everyone important know you are the new owner**. The important people that need to be informed here are not only your family and close friends, but also local council, TV licence, utility companies, etc. You should have done this during the gap between the exchange of contract and completion, but if you haven't done it yet, you need to get to it straight away.

The purpose of informing the local council is for them to set up your name in their system so that they can send you the local council tax bill. As explained before in the chapter "Money, Money, Money", whoever lives in the property will have to pay for the council tax (unless pre-agreed otherwise). So if you are moving in as the owner, you should give them your name; if you are thinking of renting it out in the future, give them your name to start with and change it afterwards; if you have a tenant already lined up to move right after the completion, then give them your tenant's name. If you are living there alone, make sure you tell them that, as you should be able to get a discount.

So how do you know which council your new property belongs to and what are their contact details? There are many ways to find out. One of the simplest ways is to type your property's postcode here in this government website link http://local.direct. gov.uk/LDGRedirect/Start.do?mode=1, press enter, then the next screen will tell you the name of the local council your property belongs to; it also gives you the website address for that council with contact details and instructions on how to pay council tax.

The next group of important people to contact are the utility companies: water, electricity, gas and TV licence. You should be able to find out the suppliers from the seller or the seller's agent or solicitor. Thames water http://www.thameswater.co.uk will be the main provider for water and sewage for the greater London area. The "Big Six" energy suppliers in Britain cover 90% share of domestic customers in terms of gas and electricity and they are British Gas, EDF Energy, Npower, E.ON UK, Scottish Power and SSE.

You don't have to stay with the previous occupant's providers. This is a great time to shop around and find the best deals for you. Set up direct debits for payments so the money is automatically paid from your bank account when it is due. This will help you keep track of your budget and avoid late-payment charges. And some utility companies may give you a discount if you pay in this way.

You also need to pay for the TV licence if you are watching TV here in the UK; again, whoever uses this service is going to pay for it. The current rate for a colour TV is £145.50 per year, and £49 for black and white TV for a year, which has been frozen by the government until 31st of March, 2017. This fee you are paying allows the BBC's UK services to remain free of advertisements and independent of shareholder and political interest.

Change your addresses if you need to. If you have already have a bank account here, a credit card, store cards, subscriptions, mobile phone bill, then you need to inform them of the change of your address if you decide to use that property as your home address in the UK. If you need to re-direct your mail, you can arrange this with Royal Mail pretty easily with a small payment. They can redirect to any UK or overseas address for 3, 6 or 12 months from £29.99 for each last name.

For more information, check their website here :
*https://www.royalmail.com/personal/receiving-mail/
redirection?PSID=Google&cid=RD0115_PPC_SM_37*

Get insured. By this stage, you should already have your building insurance in place. If not, you should have no reason for not doing it! For more information on this and the ideal time to get this done, go back to chapter seven, "The Great Expectations" and read again. Now, whether you are going to live there yourself or rent it out, I would recommend you get good contents insurance. This is not only to protect your expensive and memorable belongings within the property, but also to protect you from greater costs if water from your flat is leaking into the unit beneath yours. Check the terms and conditions as well as prices.

Well, that's pretty much everything. But what if something goes wrong three days after you've moved into the property? Or what if something breaks one

one month after your new tenant moved in? What will you do? Who is going to cover the cost and whom can you turn to for help?

Those are the million dollar questions, aren't they?

Let's have a look at who is still in the picture at this stage. Your agent? By this time, he/she has already got his/her commission, so professionally your relationship with that person is temporarily over. Whether you two will still communicate depends on your relationship, such as you have the potential to bring him/her more business or you two have become friends. Otherwise, theoretically, your agent is no longer there to help you.

How about the surveyor? They have done the survey report for you and they didn't foresee this problem. Can you go back to them? Well, it depends. If the problem should've been covered in their report and they failed their professional standards and did not point it out correctly to you, then yes, you can go back to them. For example, if the surveyor engaged failed to notice the property has serious subsidence and dampness problems and you discovered that when you moved in, and it will cost you £50,000 to make it right, then you should have a claim based on the grounds that the surveyor was negligent. He/she has missed the defects that he/she should have seen and therefore he/she has not carried out his/her instructions with reasonable skill and care. If you have solid grounds and proof, then you should be in the position to sue the surveyor for negligence and/or the company, for any liabilities. But if the surveyor has pointed out to you "There is a damp issue developing in the property" in the report, and after you moved in, the dampness condition got worse and will cost you £50,000 to repair, then it is no longer the surveyor's concern, unfortunately. 99% of the time, you will have no professional relationship or contact with the surveyor after the report is done. They were paid to carry out a specific job, and as long as they got that job done professionally, they are out of the picture.

Solicitors? For sure, they have stayed till the last minute. They even worked for you after you got your keys. Will they help you with the problems occurring in the property after you have moved in? You will be very optimistic to think so. Did you know that it is actually possible for sellers and buyers to carry out their own legal work here in the UK? Although very few people do so. The legal work mainly involved in the property transaction here is to transfer the legal title in property, which is also called "conveyancing". This can be done by solicitors or by licensed conveyancers. Licensed conveyancers are not solicitors but have legal training in the conveyancing process. For simplicity, I have been using "solicitors" throughout the book to avoid the confusion. The reason I am explaining this here is to tell you exactly what your solicitors do! Their job is to transfer the title, and to ensure the legal process of this is done correctly. Their job is not to help you with any further repair issues that you may have in the new property. Once their case is closed, their case is closed.

Who else? The seller!

If you are buying a second hand property, the chance for you to meet that person and have direct contact with him will be minimal. You will usually get a handbook or a note from that person about using certain things in the property, but that's probably it. He/she sold the property, got the money and moved on.

If your seller was a developer, then things are rather different here! Developers usually offer years of building warranty and some offer additional internal guarantees. Currently, 80% of new homes are under the NHBC 10 year warranty scheme. So what does this mean to you?

It means a lot.

When you buy a new off-plan home, don't you want the assurance that the property has been constructed in a proper manner and satisfies current construction standards? Because much of the work is not visible on completion when you were given the keys, such as the foundation, floor insulation, damp proof course, wall insulation, the pipe layout and the wire arrangement, bodies like NHBC are designed to protect the buyers of new homes. People like you.

If the properties you are buying are under the scheme, then during the construction, an inspection will be undertaken to ensure that the current standards are being achieved.

If your property is covered by the NHBC 10 year warranty, then you know in the first two years, you will be covered by them on any defect that is a result of the builder not meeting the NHBC standards. In years three to ten, you will be covered for cost over £500 for defects that are related to foundations, load bearing and non-load bearing walls, ceilings etc. If this is an area that particularly concerns you, you can find out more information here on their official website http://www.nhbc.co.uk/Homeowners/

So what does this mean to you? This means again you should do your research, that I talked about in chapter four, at the early stage of your property buying process so that you can choose a good developer that offers you a warranty like this and is regulated. You should choose a developer that has good "after-sales" customer service, as they will be the main group of people you will be dealing with for the next few years.

Also, don't forget that there are a couple of new faces in the picture now – your new insurance company and potentially your new letting agent if you choose to rent your newly purchased property out.

Theoretically, the insurance people are there to catch you when unwanted things happen, but that does not necessarily mean they will catch you every single time. You need to find out what exactly they do cover and what they don't cover, and if you are not sure about something, you need to ask. If you don't know what to ask, or what you should insure for, do some research, or write down on a piece of paper things that would really concern you when they go wrong and things that will cost you a lot of money when they go wrong. Then ask the insurance company whether these are covered before you jump into a long-term professional relationship with them. Get it right; then you will have yourself a very good friend for a long time.

If you are going to use a letting agent to rent out and manage your property, things are much easier as they will be the professional who will help you out with almost everything.

I will talk through everything in detail with you in the next chapter, but now, go organise that party and celebrate! You deserve it!

Chapter Ten
To Sell or to Let, That is the Question

We have come a long way together on this journey, haven't we? I am deeply grateful for you to have chosen this book as part of your great adventure of buying an asset in the UK! And I hope you have found the information useful, so far.

One of the reasons that I started to write this book is to help my clients and people like me, make our lives easier. As I said earlier on, when I bought my first property here in the UK, after my graduation on my first proper job, I so wished there was someone, or some book out there in my own language that I could refer to and lean on whenever I came across a problem. At that time, as a foreigner, I didn't have any close friends who had bought a property in the UK who could give me any professional advice. There was so much information out there on the internet that was incomplete that I just could not make any sense out of anything. I also found it difficult when everything was written in English and in professional terms, even though I spoke fluent English. I didn't want to ask the agent who sold me the property too many questions for fear they would sense I was just an inexperienced foreigner buyer, who did not know what she was doing, and sell me a property that they could not sell to a local experienced buyer.

Property buying was like a constant test to me. I appeared calm from the outside, but inside, I was screaming out loud every time I needed to make a decision: which solicitor to use, which property to buy, do I continue with the purchase after reading the surveyor report, who should I chase when things move slower than I expected... then after the completion of the property, I was facing another tough question: how do I let my property out? And years later, how do I sell it on?

Now that we are towards the end of this great journey, you are probably facing the same questions – how are you going to rent out your property or how are you going to sell it?

Whether you are just thinking about buying a property in the UK or you have already got the keys to your new property, this chapter will be very important to you as I will show you how the system works and what you need to do in order to take this step properly.

How to sell your property

I will start with sales – the opposite end of buying -- while your mind is still familiar with the process, as there are a lot of similarities between these two.

Also, a better understanding of the selling process will automatically help you with the buying process, wouldn't you agree?

Be prepared for some changes the moment you decide to sell your property. You are no longer the inexperienced international buyer anymore; instead, you are now officially "the vendor" (that's what we call the sellers in the property world generally) with a business to offer to the agents. You will have a new set of decisions to make at the very early stage and a few checks to write upon completion, namely your solicitor, your agent and possibly the taxman.

The first decision you need to make is not which agent to instruct. It is how you want to, or who should instruct your agent/agents.

There are two main distinctive types of agencies, depending on the way in which instructions are received; namely "sole agency", which includes joint sole agency, and "multiple agency".

If you, the vendor, decide to give instructions only to one agent for them to sell your property, then you are using the "sole agency" format. Usually, these instructions will last for a specified period of time, from a few weeks to a few months. So make sure you check the length of this period before you sign the instruction contract. Once the sole agency instructions are confirmed, any buyers must buy through the appointed agency and the agent is entitled to be paid the agreed fee by the seller.

So, why should you consider using just one agent to sell your property? What are the advantages and disadvantages of this type of instruction?

The most obvious advantage for you, the vendor, to have a "sole agency" relationship with an agent, is that you will be looking at a lower commission rate in general. For instance, if the agent charges you 2.5% for a multiple agency term, the same agent will most likely charge you 2% or lower for a sole agency term. (2% means 2% of the achieved sales price.) For a property with a high sales price tag, 0.5% can make a lot of difference. For instance, if you are selling your property at £1 million, 0.5% on commission means £5,000, which is not a small amount.

The other main advantage of "sole agency" is that you, the vendor, can build up a much better and more professional relationship with the agent. Remember what I said previously about buyers are from Mars and everyone else is from Venus? For a vendor that is not based in the UK most of the time, with limited knowledge of the market, having a strong professional relationship with your chosen agent will do you more good than bad. Think about it; your agent will be your only main contact point in the UK. Communication will be simple and direct and confusion will be reduced to a minimum! Your agent will be better able to advise on the most suitable buyer for you, and they will be more committed to you as you have put your complete trust in them for the agreed period of time. All you need to do is to follow the suggestions and advice that I have given you in the first part of this book in choosing the right agent. It could be the agent that has helped you to buy the property in the first place.

How about the downside of this type of agency term? There must be another side of the coin, mustn't there? It can't be that perfect! Ask yourself, what's the one most worrying fact about this type of agency term? And is there any way to get around it?

"You are asking us to put all our eggs in one basket!" you may think, like many of the clients that I have had before. "What if you cannot move my property in the agreed time? Then my property will be considered undesirable and even more difficult to sell!"

That is a solid concern that not only bothers you (the international vendor) but also numerous local vendors. The two most argued disadvantages of this type of agency term have been considered to be: a) sellers getting much less exposure for their property and b) the agencies are competing more to win instructions and, once achieved, there is not enough incentive to sell quickly or to obtain the maximum price as there is no competition anymore for that agreed period of time.

For you as the vendor to choose the right agent before you enter into the "sole agency" relationship, you need to know the right questions to ask to minimise these above concerns. You might want to ask them some details on how they are planning to market your property! Your property deserves a good marketing plan, great exposure to get it out there, and a good salesperson to close the deal. You want your questions to be based around those elements. See how comfortable you are with their answers before you make any decisions on which one you want to go with. You might also want to have some level of trust in their professionalism and integrity so that you know they are not just bluffing and they will deliver too.

In the sole agency term, you probably will come across something called "joint sole agents". The chance for you to actually use this type of agency is not that high, but I list it down here anyway for you to use as a reference.

"Joint sole agents" covers that situation where the two agents are working together on behalf of you, the vendor (the seller). You will only need to pay one fee and the agents usually agree between themselves how the fee will be split between them. The fee charged is usually higher than if one single agent is employed. In the above case, the same agent who offered you 2% on sole agency term, and 2.5% on multiple agency term might charge you 2.25% on the joint sole agency term. A joint sole agency may be a good solution when a property, for example, lies between two towns, giving rise to the possibility of attracting a buyer from either one. In such a situation, an agency in one town may take instructions for the property, which may be on the edge of their catchment area, and suggest the joint appointment of another agency in the adjoining town to give the best chance of finding a buyer quickly.

If you, the vendor, decided to appoint more than one agency to sell, with each agency acting independently of the others and thus in competition with one another, then you are using the "multiple agency" method.

For people that are mostly concerned about "putting all their eggs in one basket", this probably will be the best solution, as you will know that more than one agent will be marketing your property to give it more exposure (theoretically).

Instructing more than one agent will also provide you and your property with more attention as you have introduced competition into the game. Only the successful agent will be paid a fee; the unsuccessful ones receive nothing, unless there is agreement with the seller to pay some or all of their expenses, which is very unusual.

Remember I mentioned in previous chapters how the deal can fall through due to unexpected reasons? Another advantage of having multiple agents is that once a sale is agreed with one agent, if the deal falls through, you will still have the potential clients with other agents as "insurance" or "back up buyers".

Of course, all of the above advantages come at a cost as well, in addition to the very obvious one that you need to pay more commission for this type of instruction. And it is your responsibility to do your own research, know your own bottom line and be alert enough to avoid the pitfalls if you choose to use this "multiple agency term".

Ask yourself this question: if you were a buyer, and you saw a property had been advertised all over the place via a few agents, with varying picture quality, and sometimes with different prices, what would be your first impression of that property? Would you think that property was so hot, popular and a great buy that so many agents decided to sell it at the same time? Or would you think there was something wrong with the property, it was difficult to sell, and that the vendor needed a lot of help from a lot of agents to move it? Which first impression would you have? Be honest with yourself! You have been the buyer, on the other side of the table; so don't forget to think as a buyer even when your position changes.

Another potential problem you will probably face is the confusion about the commission fee payment. When you have decided to use multiple agents to act for you, you must be prepared to understand all the terms and conditions that are involved with the instruction.

I recently had a client who instructed me to sell one of his brand new properties in London, a very good unit at a quite reasonable price. I managed to find him a good cash buyer, while at the same time, one of the other five or six agents he had instructed also found him a buyer at a higher price, so understandably he went for that one instead. A week later, he called me and asked whether he could go with my client instead because for some reason, that buyer had decided to pull out.

"OK," I said to him, "I just need to confirm with my client to see whether he is still interested."

Luckily, the client still hadn't found a better option so he happily agreed to proceed.

Two days later, I got a phone call from this vendor again. "Sally, I am so sorry, I won't be able to go ahead with this anymore, I am going to take the property off the market once and for all. I need to think about what to do next."

"Why? What happened?" I knew a couple of reasons he would make this decision and his answer confirmed my initial guess.

"I should have listened to you at the beginning and should have checked the terms and conditions in the agreement. When I told one of the agents that I wanted them to remove the property from the market as I had found a buyer, they told me that they would expect the same amount of commission fees from me upon completion, as it had been put down in the sales instruction agreement that I signed. That means, if I sell this property, I need to pay two commission fees, one to you and one to them. You know I am not making that much money by selling this unit; by giving away two commissions, I am not making any financial sense here. So, I am left with no choice but to remove the property from the market or to solely rely on them to sell the property for me. At this stage, I have lost my complete trust in them."

You know sometimes how we think that things like this only happen to other people, and will never happen to us?! He was thinking exactly like that when I expressed my concerns about him instructing so many agents without having enough experience and time to understand how to control the situation.

Luckily, the market at the time was in his favor, so waiting for a few months did not do him that much damage, but imagine if you make the same mistake in a market that is less favorable to you? He was also very lucky that the agent had told him in advance about charging him; imagine they hadn't and just sent him the bill upon completion. What would he do then?

Try not to learn this lesson the hard way!

There are other downsides with this type of agency term, such as: the agents may be unlikely to devote the same time and resources to effect a sale as they would with sole agency instructions; agents would be encouraged to seek the quickest sale under the pressure of competing with other agents, which may not necessarily be on the best terms for you – the vendor.

162

"You are not helping, now." You may be thinking this by now. "You are meant to tell me what to do, which sales term I should go with, now you have told me that both of them are good, and both of them are bad. So what should I do? Shall I use the sole agency or shall I use the multiple agency?"

I wish I could simply tell you which one to go for. However, it all depends on your personal situation and also the situation of your property. The advice I can offer here is to be careful with who you instruct, how many you are instructing and read the contract before you sign anything.

Which leads to the second decision to make: whether or not to sign the contract with the instructed agent/agents.

There are many things you should look out for when given a contract by the agent you are intending to work with. Here, I am just going to show you what to check in order to avoid the mistakes the previous seller made. You should look out for **key terms** used in the contract to indicate under what circumstances you, the vendor/the seller, will have to pay commission to the estate agent.

There are three types of specific wording used in a common contract of an agency: sole agency, sole selling rights and ready, willing and able purchaser.

Sole agency means that if you the vendor find a buyer yourself, then you don't need to pay the commission fee, but if the agent finds you a buyer you will need to pay the commission even when the exchange of contract occurs outside the original agency period.

Sole selling rights means that the instructed agent will get the commission no matter who sold the property during the instructed period. That includes if you, the vendor, find someone yourself who is willing to buy the property from you; although the agent didn't do anything, they are still entitled to get paid during the sole selling rights term.

Ready, willing and able purchaser means that you, the vendor, have to pay the agent the agreed fee if a buyer is introduced who is willing and able to exchange contracts, even if you change your mind or something happens that forces you not to sell the property; you can remove the property from the market, but you will still need to pay the agent the full fee agreed.

See how important it is for you to read and understand what you are going to sign before you actually sign it?

There are a few other decisions you need to make in addition to the above two, such as deciding on the right selling price with the help of the agent, and deciding on whether you are happy with the commission rate you have been offered, etc.

However, selling a property also means there are certain responsibilities you need to take on, which can be divided into two main areas: money related and truth related.

Money related responsibilities are pretty straightforward, such as you are obliged to pay your solicitor fee, so remember to ask for a quotation before you instruct any; you need to pay the commission to the agent upon completion — usually, your solicitor will deduct that for you from the sales income and transfer the remaining amount to your account close to the completion; and you also need to pay capital gains tax if you have made a profit and it is not your prime home.

Truth related responsibilities means that it is your responsibility to provide truthful information when selling a property, such as providing honest information when filling in the property information sheet with the fixture and fittings, things you will be leaving behind upon completion, truthful information about the ownership, any related history on the property that you are aware of, etc.

For the money transfer, closer to completion, your solicitor will send you an estimated price list with all of the deductions and the final income from the property, and you will need to provide them with the details of your bank account so that they can transfer the money to the agreed account upon completion.

How to rent out your property

There are two ways for you to rent out your property: you can either be a private landlord, which means if you have the ability to do it yourself, you are absolutely allowed to rent the property and manage it yourself; or you can have a professional estate agent company handle it for you.

The majority of the international buyers choose the latter option. If you are in this category, but not sure where to start, then the following information will be particularly useful for you.

You have the options of instructing one letting agent or you can instruct multiple agents. Generally speaking, whoever finds a tenant receives the commission. Compared to the sales business, letting is pretty simple and straightforward in this way.

For a good property in a rent friendly area, if the price is right, it takes no time for a property to be rented out. It is a fast moving sector compared to sales. So, without any special circumstances, you should be OK with just instructing one or two agents; normally, you are better off if you can keep the number low.

The one decision you will need to make, though, is what type of service you require from the chosen agent. Usually, there are three choices: full management, rent collection and let only. Each comes with a different commission rate.

Full management is a one-stop service that charges you the highest rate out of the three. The ranges you are looking at usually are between 10% and 18% (depends on the area). For instance, if you are charged 15% with 10% being the letting fee and 5% for the management fee, usually that means you will need to pay 10% of the annual rental income at one go at the beginning of the tenancy, and then 5% of the monthly rental income on a monthly basis. However, the rate and payment term depends on individual companies, so make sure you understand the rate and payment terms before you enter into a professional relationship with one. Under this service, your chosen agent will look after everything for you, from marketing your property, arranging viewings, proposing an offer, helping you to decide which tenant is the best option, conducting a credit check, setting up the tenancy agreement, checking in, collecting rent on a monthly basis to full management of the property. The agent that can provide services like this will need to have a separate management team specifically looking after properties like yours. Usually there are two misunderstandings with services like this: one is that "full management" means managing everything for you. This is not the case: even with full management, there are limits. There are a lot of things that the agent will not do for you, or they will do it at a cost, such as cut an extra set of keys, so find out what services are included that might be useful to you. The other misunderstanding is that "they will fix any problems for you at their cost". Just like managing everything for you, there are limits. Let's say two days after your new tenant moved in, they reported to the management team a list of problems, such as broken door handle, blocked sink, broken washing machine, etc. Typically, the management team will report the problem to you first to make you aware of the situation. Then they will look into the problems to find out whose responsibilities they are and get a cost quote while keeping you updated. If the problem is covered by your insurance terms, they will normally sort that out for you with your permission; if the problem has to be covered by you, such as a broken washing machine which was not caused by the tenant, then they will provide you with a quote to either fix it or replace it, and you — the landlord — will need to pay the bill.

Rent collection is a service that is less comprehensive than full management; the agent will only find a tenant for you, set things up, and collect the monthly rent. They will not do any of the management duties for you. Therefore, the commission rate falls between letting only and full management.

The most basic service is the letting only, which is just what it says: the agent will only find you the tenant and you will need to collect the rent and manage the property, yourself. This type of service has the lowest commission rate among the three. Again, make sure you confirm the rate and the payment terms with the agent before you sign anything with them.

Now, I have a question for you: what is the biggest difference between renting out your property and selling it?

To which you probably will answer, "If I sell the property, I don't own it anymore; but if I rent it out, then I still own it."

Yes, that's one way of saying it, if we look at this from the ownership point of view. But, if we look at it from a monetary point of view, to sell a property means that you cash in big time at one go, while to rent it means you will have a smaller yet, ongoing income. If we look at it from a responsibility point of view, to sell a property means that your duty towards that particular property ends the moment you've completed the deal, while renting out a property means that you will have continuous responsibilities towards the tenant, your agent, and anyone that is related to this matter until the day you sell it.

So what does this mean to you in real terms?

It means that as a landlord, you have duties and responsibilities to carry out and there are rules that you need to follow. For instance, by law you are required to provide a gas safety certificate. If you fail your responsibilities and something bad happens to your tenant, you could be charged. It can be a rather serious matter, so if you are an international investor, my advice to you is to use a management company if you are not experienced or comfortable enough to do it yourself.

And just like that, you completed the first cycle of your UK property investment.

Acknowledgements

A few years ago, when I was single and searching for my second property, I met a Chinese woman at a house viewing appointment. She was single at the time as well and was looking for a place to live in. "I want to find a nice place that I can afford in a nice area, settling down, make it cozy and homely, and then I can move on to find a nice boyfriend, fall in love, bring him back home, get married and live happily ever after." I remembered how close I felt towards her upon hearing this; How shocked I felt after she told me she has been looking for the past year and half without any success; How stuck and exhausted she was feeling by carrying out all those viewings every weekend without time to even go out and socialise, let alone meeting her future partner; And how I told myself at that point that I must try everything I can to avoid her mistakes so that I can move on to the next important thing.

Three weeks later my offer for a property has been accepted, three months later, I moved in to that nice flat, four months afterwards, I met this wonderful man who later became my husband, one year later, the value of that flat has grown by close to 20% and was producing 6% of rental return for me.

It was that encounter that made me realise the importance of getting yourself ready as much as you can, equipping yourself with as much knowledge as possible, staying realistic and knowing exactly what you are looking for. That was the moment that led to further development of this book writing idea – So I suppose, before I thank anyone else, I should thank that random encounter and I do hope that she has achieved what she wanted.

Now come to the real thanks. Ruben Carbajal, the author of <The gifted Program>, thank you for giving me all that valuable advice at the very beginning of this whole process from New York City; John Biesack, very graciously and patiently proofread the whole draft in a short span of time together with those wonderful suggestions and feedback from the United States; Lord David Evans, thank you for your immense support of this project and the kind words you have put in the foreword; Alison Hurcombe, the publishing director of London Property Review South, your genuine encouragement and belief in me has given me that little push to make this happen, how funny is it that everything we do in life has an effect on other people's lives, sometimes we know it, other times we don't?

Bubbly, happy and hardworking Nikki Hamersley from the Wharf newspaper, thank you for introducing me to the professionals in the property industry to give me interviews and quotes for this book to be more practical. David Smith from Octagon Developments Limited generously gave me the benefit of his years of property expertise and offered my reader and me the most valuable advice in investing in UK properties. Mark Gawor and Polly Yu from Gawor & Co solicitors, thank you for using your weekend private time to answer my interview questions and take this whole thing very seriously.

Stephen Brown's insight and professional knowledge on mortgage matters has inevitably answered a lot of questions in the field. Thank you, Richard Evans, your generous offering of advice on the book title, cover design has a huge positive impact. Your highly efficient working attitude and professional manner also pushed me to raise up my own standards. Nia Thomas and Dara Huang – I am blessed to have known two women of such brilliance. Dara Huang, your word of "woman Power" while giving me that "high five" at that venue has pushed me one step closer to the journey I am on now; Nia Thomas, your selfless recommendations in the past 10 years have only brought good to my career. For that, you deserve a big hug. Special thank you to Edwin Chiu, the person that gave me a job before I ventured out on my own, led me into the property industry and shared his more than 20 years experience and wisdom. For friends like Yuan Yuan Sun, Nancy Tu and Ella Xun Huan Zhou, thank you for being genuinely happy for me for what I do and understanding the reasons behind this. Long Qing, the chairman for AnHui business association in UK, author of <Antique Clocks: Art and Technology in Time> who have shared his experience in editing and publishing a book.

My sincere gratitude towards Ms Mei Lu, the co-founder of Lu Oliphant for sharing her professionally written articles on the legal matters related to property buying process;

A special word of gratitude is also due to John and Lesley Hammond from Property TV, who have given their time and effort to proofread my draft and bear the pain of correcting a great many of the grammar and spelling mistakes that I have made! Finally, my parents, my beloved husband and our dog Snowy, thank you for providing me with such a loving family and nurturing me with your untouchable belief, 100% of support and unconditional love. For that, I am deeply grateful. Thank you.

Resources
(Alphabetical Order)

Abode 2 – www.abode2.com
UK's fastest growing luxury property magazine
focusing exclusively on the finest residential homes
and premium developments across the globe. A must-
have read for anyone serious about buying in the UK
or overseas. www.abode2.com

ACE Funding - www.acefunding.org
Founded by Hon Richard Evans, ACE connects
funders with a diverse range of property development
opportunities in London, the South East and selected
areas country wide that require funding with family
offices, investment managers and direct to UHNW'S.

DHLiberty – www.dhliberty.com
Founded by Dara Huang, the daughter of a NASA
scientist and a Harvard Graduate. DHLiberty is a fast
growing international, award winning architecture
and interior practice. It's based in central London
with representation in HongKong and Shanghai.

Gawor and Co Solicitors – www.gawor.com
Been the only firm of solicitors in Wapping for over 15 years, Gawor & Co solicitors are specialist property solicitors in East London Docklands.

London Property Review South Magazine – www.londonpropertyreview.co.uk
Firmly established as south London's leading property-focused monthly magazine, it delivers a magnificent selection of the finest and most exclusive homes currently on the market to AB residential addresses with circulation of 45,000 and a readership of 112,000.

LuOliphant Solicitors LLP – www.luoliphant.com
Founded in 1999, Lu Oliphant Solicitors LLP has become one of the steadily growing legal firms in London. The company works to provide an environment that fosters a strongly bonded team of lawyers, all of whom are able to work together to provide dedicated client care. Their skilled legal experts are trilingual (English, plus French, Mandarin and Cantonese) and have a track record of providing exceptional advice on multifarious legal issues for clients in the UK, China and globally.Equipped with a very experienced conveyancing team, LuOliphant can spot issues in good time and deal with the matter to clients' satisfaction before exchange.

Nabarro LLP - www.nabarro.com
With offices in London, Brussels, Dubai, Manchester, Sheffield and Singapore, this international law firm delivers the highest quality, business-focused advice to clients, clearly and concisely, no matter how complex the situation. Its core practice areas include Corporate/Commercial, Real Estate, Dispute Resolution and Infrastructure, Construction and Energy and it specialises in the Healthcare, Infrastructure, Real Estate and Technology sectors. The firm has longstanding relationships with a network of selected firms worldwide for cross-border work. This includes the Broadlaw Group, a strategic

alliance with partner firms in France, Germany, Italy and Spain creating a network of more than 1,000 lawyers based in 27 cities across Europe, Asia, the Middle East and North Africa

Octagon Development Ltd. - www.octagon.co.uk
Founded in 1980, Octagon is a British, privately owned company, which develop prestigious homes throughout London and the Home Counties. Over three decades Octagon have established an enviable reputation, for which they have received well over one hundred awards for their outstanding quality and design skills.

Property TV – http://www.propertytelevision.tv
Privately owned by a group of businessmen with appropriate backgrounds in TV broadcasting, the Internet, and the property industry. The TV channel launched on the BSKYB platform and on the tvcatchup app in the summer of 2015. Property TV provides entertainment and information about property and the property industry while also providing the next generation of property searches using TV and Internet broadcasting to make both searching and selling properties easier and a more enjoyable experience.

The Wharf Newspaper – www.wharf.co.uk
As the leading newspaper in Canary Wharf and Docklands, it has been publishing weekly since 1998.